The Akkadian Empire

A Captivating Guide to the First Ancient Empire of Mesopotamia and How Sargon the Great of Akkad Conquered the Sumerian City-States

© Copyright 2022

All Rights Reserved. No part of this book may be reproduced in any form without permission in writing from the author. Reviewers may quote brief passages in reviews.

Disclaimer: No part of this publication may be reproduced or transmitted in any form or by any means, mechanical or electronic, including photocopying or recording, or by any information storage and retrieval system, or transmitted by email without permission in writing from the publisher.

While all attempts have been made to verify the information provided in this publication, neither the author nor the publisher assumes any responsibility for errors, omissions or contrary interpretations of the subject matter herein.

This book is for entertainment purposes only. The views expressed are those of the author alone, and should not be taken as expert instruction or commands. The reader is responsible for his or her own actions.

Adherence to all applicable laws and regulations, including international, federal, state and local laws governing professional licensing, business practices, advertising and all other aspects of doing business in the US, Canada, UK or any other jurisdiction is the sole responsibility of the purchaser or reader.

Neither the author nor the publisher assumes any responsibility or liability whatsoever on the behalf of the purchaser or reader of these materials. Any perceived slight of any individual or organization is purely unintentional.

Free Bonus from Captivating History (Available for a Limited time)

Hi History Lovers!

Now you have a chance to join our exclusive history list so you can get your first history ebook for free as well as discounts and a potential to get more history books for free! Simply visit the link below to join.

Captivatinghistory.com/ebook

Also, make sure to follow us on Facebook, Twitter and Youtube by searching for Captivating History.

Contents

INTRODUCTION 1
CHAPTER 1 – SUMERIAN CRADLE OF CIVILIZATION 3
CHAPTER 2 – THE LEGEND OF SARGON THE GREAT 11
CHAPTER 3 – BUILDING AN EMPIRE 20
CHAPTER 4 – ENHEDUANNA...30
CHAPTER 5 – THE SONS OF SARGON 40
CHAPTER 6 – NARAM-SIN TAKES THE EMPIRE TO SOARING HEIGHTS AND TRAGIC DEPTHS 48
CHAPTER 7 – TRUTHS WRAPPED IN FICTION: "THE LEGEND OF CUTHA" AND "THE CURSE OF AGADE"..56
CHAPTER 8 – THE EPIC GILGAMESH 66
CHAPTER 9 – "A MIGHTY HUNTER IN OPPOSITION TO GOD"............85
CHAPTER 10 – END OF THE EMPIRE..95
CONCLUSION...100
HERE'S ANOTHER BOOK BY CAPTIVATING HISTORY THAT YOU MIGHT LIKE 103
FREE BONUS FROM CAPTIVATING HISTORY (AVAILABLE FOR A LIMITED TIME) 104
REFERENCES 105

Introduction

One after another, strange objects began appearing on the tables of Middle Eastern marketplaces in the 1920s. They contained strange, almost alien-looking symbols that no vendors or shoppers had ever seen before. Those symbols weren't alien—they were from a civilization that had been lost up until the 1880s. They were symbols of an ancient empire. No, not Egypt. They were from a much older empire that had an even greater impact on history.

The symbols, which we now know as cuneiform writing, were from not only the first known empire but also one of the first known civilizations—the Sumerians. The rise of the Akkadian Empire, which united the Semites and the Sumerians, was a stark turning point in Mesopotamian history. Its influence would echo throughout the centuries and cultures, influencing conquerors and world powers alike.

For hundreds of years, the Akkadians, who were predominately Semitic, and the Sumerians lived side by side. Although they shared certain common cultural traditions, the neighboring peoples were often at odds. Rulers had tried to unite the peoples of the region with limited success until a legendary king of unknown origin showed up on the scene.

Within the time period of the empire, art, architecture, trade, and urbanization rose to new heights. But unfortunately, so did rebellions and wars—something that became a common theme throughout the empire's history.

The empire, however, is so ancient that few written historical accounts survive from the time. Clay inscriptions dug up by archaeologists give us a glimpse into the culture, the empire, and the men who ruled it. The famed *Sumerian King List* helps us to know who ruled, but details and dates remain somewhat elusive. Interestingly, a lot of what we know about the people and the culture comes from the literary works that were left behind, some of which have become epic tales that are well known today.

To understand the Akkadian Empire, it is important to learn about the Sumerian culture from which it stemmed. This book will dedicate some time to discuss the Sumerians and their impact on civilization and the Akkadian Empire. It will also discuss Sargon the Great. Where did he come from, who was he, and why was "great" added to his title?

Also, how did the Akkadian Empire even start? Why was it in a near-constant state of war? How did the empire meet its end at the hands of a less developed civilization? And how did climate change play a part in the downfall of the empire? We will also dive into the epic "naru" literature and talk about the legendary Gilgamesh and a mysterious "villain" whose true identity has eluded scholars and historians for thousands of years.

Chapter 1 – Sumerian Cradle of Civilization

Thousands of years ago, a civilization emerged from between two great, life-sustaining rivers, the Euphrates and the Tigris. This region is often called the "cradle of civilization," and Sumer was located in a region that the ancient Greeks called Mesopotamia, today known as southern Iraq.[1]

For the most part, the origins of the Sumerians are a mystery, but their civilization was a powerhouse of science, mathematics, engineering, architecture, and art, as well as the birthplace of the first written language. Stories from the civilization, both true and fictionalized, live on as legends thousands of years later. Their knowledge, culture, and system of writing were the foundations of an empire—the Akkadian Empire.

---

[1] Translated to mean "land between two rivers."

An artist depiction of the ancient city of Uruk.

We know these ancient people as Sumerians, but they called themselves Saggiga, meaning either "black-headed" or "bald-headed ones." Though they shared a common region, writing system, and ancestry (likely Semitic), the Sumerians were not a cohesive civilization.[2] Sumer was made up of numerous city-states, with most of them being their own sovereign entity. Each would have a king of its own. But evidence shows that there were not just kings but perhaps at least one ruling queen as well.

Not a lot is known about Queen Puabi, but she was a Semitic Akkadian and an important person in the region, perhaps the first known woman to rule in her own right.[3] When her tomb was uncovered, it was a trove of information and literal treasures. From it, we can glean information about her civilization and culture, as well as what a royal ruler at that time might be like.

Though archaeologists call her a "queen," the clay cylinder seals pinned to the royal robes still enshrouding her dead body identify her by the title "nin" or "eresh."[4] These Sumerian words mean "queen"

---

[2] Semitic people were descendants of the biblical Shem, the son of Noah. Ancient Israelites and modern-day Jews identify with the Semitic race.

[3] She would have ruled before the rise of the Akkadian Empire.

[4] Cylinder seals were used by royalty to show identity, title, and status. They were also often used as official seals and stamps.

and "priestess." Either way, she was definitely an important person in a high position. Given that seals were ancient status symbols of the time and that Puabi had three, possibly from when she was a princess, these point toward her being queen.

Evidence of how high her status was can be seen in the illustrations of the seals as well. She is depicted with an overflowing food pantry, eating rich delicacies like leg of lamb, and drinking wine and beer—interestingly enough through a straw. The robed Puabi has male and female servants by her side, and female musicians entertain the queen and her dinner guests.

Close-up of one of the three cylinder seals found in Queen Puabi's tomb.

There was, however, one thing notably missing from her seals that almost all other ancient women had—a mention of a husband. The fact that there was no mention of a husband or a king indicates she probably ruled on her own, which is quite a surprising find since these ancient societies were patriarchal. As surprising as it was, what was found in her tomb was even more stunning.

Queen Puabi was found in the Royal Cemetery at Ur dressed for the afterlife in incredible royal regalia.[5] A magnificent headdress of golden leaves and flowers encircled her head, and she was adorned with jewelry and accessories made up of precious metals and stones like gold, silver, and lapis lazuli. Her body was covered in an elaborate cloak of lapis lazuli and carnelian beads.

Queen Puabi's headdress and jewelry.

The splendor did not stop there. What she took to the "afterlife" was a treasure mostly seen in movies. Besides ornate jewelry and belts, Queen Puabi was buried with a superbly crafted lyre, a gold and lapis lazuli bull's head, golden plates, flatware, drinking vessels, and, most

---

[5] Considered by some the richest and most spectacular royal cemetery ever found

incredibly, a chariot decorated with silver lioness' heads. Aside from the glitz and wealth, there was another shocking discovery within the tomb that tells us a great deal about the culture.

Queen Puabi was not sent into the "afterlife" alone. The chariot buried with her was attended by horses and lions. Puabi also had human attendants buried with her in order to attend to their queen in the netherworld. Archaeologists found fifty-two servants in all. They would have been sacrificed, either willingly or unwillingly.[6] The first archaeologists who found the tomb believed the attendants poisoned themselves in order to join their queen in death, but newer technology reveals that they met violent ends. CAT scans done by researchers at the University of Pennsylvania Museum of Archaeology and Anthropology found that the attendants had shatter patterns on their skulls, indicating that they had been struck in the head, perhaps with a small hammer-like tool, which was also found in the pit. It is unknown how the queen herself died, but she offers a rare glimpse into the world that was.

Aside from a look into one monarch's life, we also have a broader picture of how the people lived at the time. Although the region was disparate, the Sumerian civilization had a capital—the great walled city of Ur. Ur and some of the other larger, wealthier cities were quite advanced, especially for what we think of when it comes to ancient civilizations. They had public buildings, marketplaces, workshops, and, in some cases like in Ur, a form of indoor plumbing to draw and store water.

Religion was an integral part of the civilization; the people literally built their lives around it. Each city-state had its own patron god or goddess, which the people believed protected the city and ruled over their affairs from the heavens. A ziggurat, or pyramid-like temple,

---

[6] There were other so-called "death pits" around Queen Puabi, but there is no evidence that links them directly with her. They may have been burial pits belonging to other royals.

dominated the landscape of each city, making it impossible for eyes not to be drawn to its immense size and significance.

One of the most famous and outstanding of these was the Ziggurat of Ur. It was three stories high! It wasn't the peaked pyramids we think of when we picture the ancient Middle East. Ramps and graduated terraces led to a flattened top. A temple to the local god was on this level, which was closest to the heavens. These great complexes were more than just temples, though. They also served as priestly homes and ceremonial palaces, which was appropriate considering many of the kings claimed some form of divinity. But a closer look at the ziggurats tells us more about the beliefs of these ancient people, and we can see recurring themes that were adopted by later civilizations and cultures, even those far from their origin.

Ziggurat of Ur before and after restoration

The moon god Nanna was the patron god of Ur. The Sumerians believed that their gods dwelled in the eastern mountains of Elam, similar to how the ancient Greeks believed their gods lived on Mount Olympus. In order for the gods to do their job and protect their cities, the deities needed to keep close at hand. The ziggurats, with their hill-like shapes, were local representations of those faraway mountains, giving their patron deity a familiar "home" in the city in which to dwell. Since the people often attributed human-like traits to the deities, it made sense to them that they would have human-like needs as well. Tending to these would need to be given the highest priority.

The ziggurats had it all. Kitchens and storehouses were right at hand in order for priests to make and serve food to their god. Nanna and the other gods even had their own bedchambers on top of the ziggurat—a comfortable place for them to reside. In addition, a maiden from the city was chosen to live there; she would be given as a companion to the patron god or goddess.

Although religion heavily influenced their lives, the Sumerians were very busy with inventions and innovations. Besides creating one of the earliest known forms of writing, cuneiform, they used that writing to create epic literature, some of which still survives.[7] They also wrote down their history on a clay tablet known as the *Sumerian King List*, which claims that some of its rulers were in power an inhumanly long time—one was said to be in power as long as 1,560 years! Despite the questionable veracity of some of its claims, it remains an insightful piece of history that has lasted thousands of years.

---

[7] Cuneiform consists of wedge-shaped symbols pressed into wet clay with a specialized stylus.

An example of cuneiform.

Sumerians were also busy developing a time system based on the number sixty—the very system we still use today. They also created the lunar calendar, which is still in use by some cultures. They made life easier by inventing the plow, and they made travel easier (and more fun) by inventing a primitive form of the sailboat.

The legacy of the Sumerians has rippled down into modern times in some aspects, but their influence on the successive and surrounding cultures was very great. So, when King Lugal-zage-si of Umma loosely united the city-states of Sumer between 2375 and 2350 BCE, everything was falling into place. The makings of an empire were already in play.

Chapter 2 – The Legend of Sargon the Great

My mother was a changeling, my father I knew not,

The brother of my father loved the hills,

My home was in the highlands, where the herbs grow.

My mother conceived me in secret, she gave birth to me in concealment.

She set me in a basket of rushes,

She sealed the lid with tar.

She cast me into the river, but it did not rise over me,

The water carried me to Akki, the drawer of water.

He lifted me out as he dipped his jar into the river,

He took me as his son, he raised me,

He made me his gardener.

–The Legend of Sargon, found at the Library of Ashurbanipal in the ruins of ancient Nineveh[8]

---

[8] It is the only record of Sargon's origin, so much is unknown about his early life before the formation of the empire.

In the king's palace in the sterling city of Kish, the monarch had begun to grow suspicious of his most trusted servant, a man who had risen from obscurity to become the second-most powerful person in the city-state. His father, who perhaps was a traitor or someone of low status, appears to have never known his son.[9] His mother, possibly a priestess or a woman of status, chose to abandon the child she secretly bore.

After putting him in a waterproof reed basket, his mother put him in the waters of the Euphrates River and pushed him out into the current, letting it carry him downstream to wherever fate might take him. A palace employee in Kish, a man named Akki, had gone down to the river to collect water when he saw the basket. Perhaps he heard the child's pathetic cries, or perhaps he was just curious to see what was in the mysterious basket. But when he found the child, he took him home and raised him as his own.

The boy grew up around the palace where his adopted father worked, and when he grew old enough, he became employed as a gardener for the king. But this gardener perhaps did not feel that managing plants was all he was destined to do. Claiming that he had the love and backing of the goddess Ishtar, he began to work his way up through the royal court, gaining status and reaching higher and higher until he stood next to King Ur-Zababa as his cupbearer.[10]

His title of cupbearer did not mean he was merely a server or glorified royal waiter; it was far greater and more important of a position than that.[11] He carried the king's seal and had the authority to give approval on the monarch's behalf. Anyone who wanted an audience with Ur-Zababa had to see his cupbearer first, and the cupbearer would determine whether that person would be allowed to

---

[9] A text fragment from the legend names his father as La'ibum.
[10] Some texts of the legend seem to indicate that Ur-Zababa appointed the cupbearer after a dream, but it does not state why.
[11] There are no Sumerian writings that detail the exact duties of the king's cupbearer. However, the information presented is based on records of Assyrian (a related civilization) cupbearers who served not too long after.

see the king or not. The cupbearer's power was so great that he was required to taste all of the king's food and drink—not to make sure someone else hadn't poisoned it but to prove that he himself had not poisoned it in a bid to grab power. But all the power, trust, and tests of loyalty did not stop this cupbearer from secretly planning his own empire.

Meanwhile, King Lugal-zage-si, the ruler of Umma, was sweeping through Sumer in a path of conquest.[12] He sought to unite the disparate city-states throughout the region, and he had the most successful military campaign to date. His plan was working, and aside from gaining power, he would also gain control over much sought-after fertile soil and water sources. Down went the city of Lagash, which was followed by the conquest of the great city of Uruk. Eventually, only Kish in all its glory remained unbothered.

Kish was unconquered because Lugal-zage-si had agreed to leave it untouched, but after his victories over other great cities, the temptation to take Kish was too great. Believing that his god, Enlil, was with him, Lugal-zage-si started to march toward Kish.

One night, Sargon supposedly had a disturbing dream that caused him to groan and gnaw at the ground. When Ur-Zababa heard about it, he called Sargon to him. Wanting to know what distressed him, he asked, "Cupbearer, was a dream revealed to you in the night?" He told Ur-Zababa what he saw. "There was a young woman [the goddess of war, Inanna] who was as high as the heavens and as broad as the earth. She was as firmly set as the base of a wall. For me, she drowned you in a great river, a river of blood."

Frightened, Ur-Zababa saw this dream as a warning that his most trusted servant would betray him. He told his chancellor that he believed the goddess Inanna would protect him from this potential assassination by drowning Sargon in the river but that he was not going

---

[12] Lugal was actually a title, like king or ruler, rather than a name.

to leave anything to chance. He decided he had to get rid of the cupbearer, but he didn't want to dirty his hands with the job.

He ordered his chief metalsmith, Belis-tikal, to murder the cupbearer and even detailed how to do it, telling him, "When the cupbearer has delivered my bronze hand-mirror to you, throw them [mirror and cupbearer] into the mold like statues."[13]

Eventually, the cupbearer was sent to deliver the bronze mirror to the smith. After he left the palace, Inanna blocked his way, telling him he was not allowed to go to the house of the smith, thus preventing the assassination.

When the cupbearer returned to the palace ten days later and appeared before the king, Ur-Zababa was shocked with fright. He knew what it meant for him, but he didn't tell anyone else. He knew he had to find another way to eliminate this threat.

When Ur-Zababa was informed that Lugal-zage-si's army was nearing the city gates, a great fear overtook him. He "sprinkled his legs" and became like a "fish floundering in brackish water." He and his city were staring down war and conquest on top of fears that his trusted second-in-command had become traitorous.[14]

Ur-Zababa saw another opportunity to rid himself of his cupbearer without dirtying his own hands. After having peace negotiations written on a clay tablet, he gave it to his cupbearer to deliver to Lugal-zage-si. However, there was another message to the enemy king imprinted on the tablet—a request to murder the man who delivered it. He wanted Lugal-zage-si to perform the assassination. The enemy king refused,[15] instead continuing his march on the city.[16]

---

[13] A mold is an extremely hot, fired foundry where metal is liquified and molded.

[14] There is no concrete evidence to support whether this was true or not or why Ur-Zababa harbored these suspicions. All we have is the legend about the dream, which cannot be verified.

[15] This part of the story, the request to murder the cupbearer, may be apocryphal.

When Lugal-zage-si and his army breached the city and triumphantly marched through its streets, Ur-Zababa knew it was over. He fled, hoping to save his own life. His cupbearer did not go with him. In fact, the man was nowhere to be found.

The cupbearer, however, had not disappeared. Instead of murdering him, Lugal-zage-si invited Sargon to join him in going up against the city he had called home just about his entire life. Lugal-zage-si unintentionally was giving him a stepping stone toward grabbing power, and Sargon would not let that slip by. He entered Kish with Lugal-zage-si and enjoyed the victory over his former king.

Victory stele showing Sargon.

---

[16] Although almost certainly untrue, later Assyrian accounts say that Lugal-zage-si's wife offered the cupbearer her "femininity as a shelter," suggesting that he was sexually irresistible and that the two had carried out some sort of affair.

Sargon saw the disaster that had befallen his city as an opportunity, and he made plans to grab it. While Lugal-zage-si remained in Kish, triumphantly celebrating his victory, the cupbearer reunited the soldiers of Kish. It is not known what his relationship with Ur-Zababa's army was like, but if he had been carefully nurturing its loyalty, this was the perfect time to put it to use.

The cupbearer, who was apparently loyal to no one, would end up following in Lugal-zage-si's footsteps, for he would continue the conquest of other city-states. However, he was not simply content with taking control over Sumer; he wanted to conquer the known world.

He would start by striking at the heart of Lugal-zage-si's conquests—Uruk. Taking the city by complete surprise while Lugal-zage-si reveled in Kish, the cupbearer and his army "laid waste to the city." He destroyed its "wall and fought with the men of Uruk and conquered them."[17]

When Lugal-zage-si heard about the conquest of Uruk, he and his army rushed out of Kish to put a stop to this usurpation of power. Except he found that the cupbearer and his army were waiting for him in the field outside the walls of Uruk.

Sargon and his army captured Lugal-zage-si and took him prisoner. But this was not enough—they wanted to thoroughly humiliate the captured conqueror. Putting an animal yoke around his neck and chaining his arms and legs, they paraded him through the city of Nippur, forcing him to march through the gate dedicated to Enlil—the very god Lugal-zage-si had credited with his victories. As he walked, the curse that Urukagina, King of Lagash, had uttered when his city

---

[17] This is according to victory inscriptions written by Sargon himself.

was defeated may have rung through his ears: "May his goddess Nisaba make him carry his sin upon his neck."[18]

A stele that includes an image of Sargon leading a procession. (Credit: Wikimedia Commons)

Immediately following his victory over Lugal-zage-si, the cupbearer pronounced himself king and took on a new name, "Sargon," meaning "legitimate king" or "rightful ruler."[19] He took over a kingdom that had been loosely united by Lugal-zage-si, and he was determined to expand it into an empire.[20]

The original legend and other early texts of Sargon's rise to power read like a mythological story. It is probably no accident that it was written that way, as it was originally written by Sargon himself.[21] There are themes in the story common to the literature of the time,

---

[18] Confusingly, the *Sumerian King List* records Lugal-zage-si and Ur-Zababa as being several generations apart. One explanation for this is that Ur-Zababa was not "drowned in a river of blood" as the dream had foretold but went back to live at the palace in Kish after his defeat. However, the Akkadian custom was to execute defeated kings. The ultimate fate of Ur-Zababa is unknown.

[19] There is no record of what his name actually was up until this point. Sargon's birth name remains unknown. There is also no record of his name as Akki's son or the name he used when he was a cupbearer.

[20] Experts have concluded that his rule may have begun in 2334 BCE, but that estimate might be off by as many as two hundred years. So, the exact date and year of his ascension to power is unknown and unconfirmed.

[21] Other texts on Sargon were later written by Assyrian rulers who proudly considered him their great predecessor. Embellishing accounts of Sargon would therefore make them appear great as well, so they had a lot of impetus to add or flesh out his manliness and other appealing aspects of his story.

particularly the interactions and interventions between deities and humans. Religion was central to the culture, and someone backed by the deities was seen as powerful. That is why kings of the period started to claim that their rulership was inherited and passed down to them directly from the heavens. It would be hard for anyone to dispute or try to overthrow authority sanctioned and imbued by the gods. But there was one thing that separated Sargon's story from those who came before him.

Rulers and conquerors before Sargon had also claimed divine backing; that was nothing new to the people they ruled. But there was an ancient elitist idea that separated the people from their ruler—how could one truly feel loyalty for a ruler who was handed everything and enjoyed divine favor that most could only dream about? Sargon created what might have been the first rags to riches story. He claimed to be from a humble background—he was abandoned by his mother, raised by a working parent, started out as a laborer, and climbed his way up the ranks. These were the ingredients that made him a relatable, sympathetic, and even likable character, despite his penchant for betrayal, war, and conquest.

That's not to say that the legend isn't factual—much of it might even be true. However, there is no evidence, at least for the most part. The whole "sent down the river in a basket" part may raise some questioning eyebrows. Some see it as metaphorical, given the beliefs of the time. Ancient Mesopotamians believed that the lands of the living and the dead were separated by a river and that crossing a river had implications of leaving the land of the living for the afterlife.[22] It could also be symbolic of transformation. Sargon had survived some sort of ordeal as an abandoned child, and he was brought by destiny to the man who found him, asserting his change from worthlessness to

---

[22] Ancient Mesopotamians had a method of testing whether someone was guilty or innocent of a crime, which they called "the Ordeal." A person accused of a crime was thrown into the river or jumped in on their own. If they survived, they were innocent; if they died, they were guilty and had received their just punishment. It is an example of their views on the river, life, and death.

worthiness. Whether it was true or not is hard to say. Often-fictionalized biographies came to be considered the truth, and even thousands of years later, no one is the wiser.

You might have noticed that his story echoes that of the biblical Moses, who was found in a reed basket on the Nile by an Egyptian princess. To many Christians, this story is widely accepted as true. There is also no evidence contradicting Sargon's version of his story, so although parts may have been romanticized (such as a goddess falling in love with him), it is accepted, for the most part, as the truth.

But true or embellished, Sargon knew how to win the people over. A story like that would only help his cause. How Sargon built the rest of his empire, however, is better recorded and more founded in fact. And that story is quite legendary.

Chapter 3 – Building an Empire

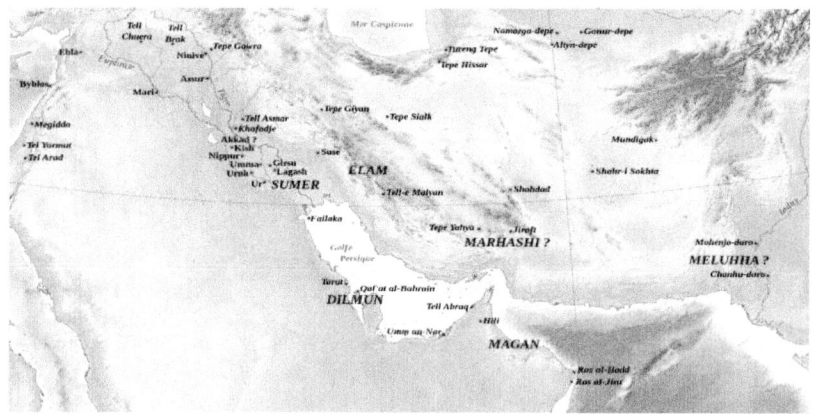

A map of the Akkadian Empire.

After conquering the cities of Sumer, which were clustered within a relatively small area, Sargon saw that there was not enough glory in that. After all, Lugal-zage-si had basically done the same thing; Sargon's victories were less than groundbreaking. But what he did next actually *was* groundbreaking, as it was a complete turn from the traditions of past kings.

In order to strive for greater glories, Sargon needed a base, a capital from which to launch his empire-building campaigns into far-flung regions. He settled on building (or possibly even rebuilding) the city of Agade, known in Hebrew as Akkad (Accad).[23] Building a city itself was no big deal, but when a king conquered another city, he did so for the glory of his home city. He would also bring the riches and resources of the conquered nations back to his home city to further its wealth. But not Sargon.

Sargon captured glory, riches, and cities for one reason only—himself. He did not do it to benefit any particular city that already existed. So, he built one for himself.[24]

Once his city was built, Sargon set his sights beyond Mesopotamia. After creating the first standing (professional) army known in history, he took his 100,000 trained fighters and crossed the Tigris River and the rugged terrain of the eastern mountains into Elam, a place no Sumerian army had ever gone.

Moving easily and with incredible speed, likely because they left the cumbersome war wagons behind since they would have trouble crossing the rugged terrain, the army used basic yet effective "shock and awe" tactics.[25] In the first wave of each attack, missiles, such as arrows, darts, or stones, were launched upon the enemy from a distance. After the initial barrage, the spearman charged. Once their spears had been used up, they took out their axes for close-quarter combat. The third and final wave, the reinforcements, ran in with their axes ready, backing up the first troops. By structuring the army into looser battle formations and using a variety of weapons, the

---

[23] The ruins of Akkad have never been found, so an exact location is difficult to pinpoint. But by using ancient documents from other cities in the area, scholars have been able to get an educated idea of its general location. It is likely north of Kish between the Tigris and Euphrates Rivers, near modern-day Baghdad.

[24] Much of the information that makes Sargon seem like an all-conquering hero is from the legend that he probably wrote himself. Some historians believe that the more likely scenario is a bit different—he took power in Kish and acted as a vassal governor for Lugal-zage-si. Perhaps Lugal-zage-si felt Sargon was getting too ambitious and wanted too much power. War really did break out at Uruk, and it is generally believed that Lugal-zage-si, after being abandoned by some of his vassal kings, was defeated and taken through the Enlil gate.

[25] If they used any of the battle vehicles as depicted in some Akkadian art and texts, it was smaller, more mobile two- and four-wheeled vehicles.

Akkadians outmatched their enemies in mobility and adaptability.[26] Records also indicate that the Akkadians may have used lions in battle; lions were a symbol of the goddess Ishtar. This would have made their army a fierce sight to behold.

Thus, Sargon conquered King Awan and the three other leaders of Elam and their cities, bringing them under Akkadian control. He continued north toward the Caspian Sea, capturing lands of various Semitic tribes like the fiercely wild and nomadic Amorites.

He and his army then turned west and continued conquering past the Tigris and all the way through the famed cedar forests of Lebanon to the sapphire waters of the Mediterranean Sea. From there, by his account, Sargon crossed the sea and conquered the island nation of Cyprus. Once back on the mainland, he and his army pushed farther north, conquering lands all the way to the silver heights of the Taurus Mountains in Turkey. By then, Sargon must have been feeling fairly invincible. He issued a challenge: "Now, any king who wants to call himself my equal, wherever I went, let him go."

He pressed his armies to continue farther west, deeper into Anatolia (Asia Minor), but it was here that Sargon hit the metaphorical wall. After thirty-four battles, his men had had enough. They were tired of war and tired of being away from home and their families. They were unable to share and enjoy the riches and glory they had attained on their campaigns. The army mutinied and refused to go on. They had taken Sargon as far as he was going to go, and now he had no choice but to turn back. Forcing the men to continue against their will, past their limits, would not preserve their much-needed loyalty to him. So, Sargon returned home.

After his victories in the south and those in the north, Sargon is said to have washed his weapons in the "Upper and Lower Seas" (the Mediterranean Sea and the Persian Gulf). This was largely symbolic, a

---

[26] This military strategy was so effective that it was used all the way up to the time of Alexander the Great.

ritual cleansing. It signified that he had reached the "end of the world" and that there was nothing left to conquer—he had taken it all.

Sargon's military campaign, however, had not been all mayhem, carnage, and the piling up of bodies (as often depicted in Akkadian reliefs). He served the people as a protector and reformer as well. In Asia Minor, the people of Purushkhanda sent him a message asking for his help against their cruel and oppressive king, Nur-daggal, who laughed at the idea that Sargon would bother to show up and help. But when Sargon and his army blasted through the city gate,[27] he was seen as a hero to those who had called upon him.[28] No matter how much truth there is to that story, he was seen as a savior to the oppressed.

He smartly stabilized his vast new empire by making sure it was unified, well organized, and well connected. This meant constructing roads and making crucial trade routes more accessible. He secured major trade routes on land and by sea, even claiming to have sent ships as far as India. With those all-important trade routes under his control, Sargon had the wealth of various parts of Mesopotamia within his reach. His trade route system also paved the way for wood and precious metals to be sent down the rivers to Akkad. A new standard for weights and measures was established, along with a state-run tax system that would keep local corruption to a minimum. He kept the corners of the empire in touch by establishing a postal system. Under Sargon, the empire also became united under one official language—Akkadian. He brought a variety of languages, cultures, and lands under the umbrella of one empire and one supreme ruler.

It appears that Sargon strove to be a ruler that showed concern for and protected his people. Now that the war for the empire was over, he wanted to protect the peace. Whenever possible, he negotiated

---

[27] The account, recorded in the story "Sargon, King of Battle," says that they "widened the gate by two acres."

peace treaties instead of continuing to war. He improved irrigation, helping to prevent drought and famine. As any good ruler would do, he made sure that the weak, particularly widows and orphans, were protected. It was said that "no one in Sumer had to beg for food."

However, there were some major obstacles for a newly installed imperial king to contend with. Sweeping through territory like a conquering juggernaut on the battlefield was one thing; maintaining control of conquered lands after the fact was quite another. Since the reaches of his empire were so vast, and transportation and information were slow to move across it, how could he keep the empire running the way he wanted? Could he trust the conquered leaders to continue ruling as loyal vassals? His predecessors had thought so, but they also hadn't been able to pull off an empire.

He once again spearheaded a new way of doing things, breaking the old order and creating a new one of his own. But these reforms did not go over well. The common working-class people of the empire admired him. To them, he was a heroic liberator and a masterful reformer. The ruling elite, however, did not have such rose-tinted glasses. He treated the people of the kingdom well enough, but he ran rather roughshod over the ruling class. He often completely replaced the existing officials, priests, and royals with Akkadian leaders fiercely loyal to him alone and not to their home city or the previous royal family. The move made perfect sense in terms of political strategy and security, but to the Sumerians, it was like a sledgehammer shattering their established institutions.

That's not to say that Sargon eliminated or assassinated royal families in all the city-states he conquered; that would create more bad will than he needed. Live royal hostages, living as "guests" in what was formerly their own palaces, were more valuable for ensuring the good

---

[28] His actions for the city were likely not completely unselfish. The area was known to be abundant in silver, a prize that would have likely appealed to the king.

behavior of their home cities. Sargon touted this concession he bestowed on them as an honor.

Besides losing high positions, there were other reasons the conquered Sumerians were offended. They hadn't achieved their positions through merit and hard work; they believed they were divinely appointed by the gods. Royals came into their positions by the right of bloodline inheritance. Dismissing the Sumerian rulers was an affront to those rights, and no matter how fair Sargon was in other matters, this type of sacrilege could not be tolerated.

The loss of their positions was bad enough, but they also lost the perks that went along with it, namely their land and side income from crops and temple revenues. Now, Sargon wanted to give these to the new Akkadian leaders he had installed. It was a shrewd move. Giving the officials a stake (land and income) in the success of the city they ruled, they were more likely to do their job in a way that ensured success. They would also remain loyal to the emperor. So, the old Sumerian royals, officials, and priests were forced to hand over their land or else face dire consequences. Even though they were offered generous compensation for doing so, it was more insulting than anything else.

Another problem was that Sargon came in and changed the official language to Akkadian. However, almost everyone spoke the Sumerian language. Imagine someone taking over the country where you were born and raised and suddenly changing all the books, schools, and spoken messages into a language you don't know or understand. The Sumerians were understandably angry. It was not a change they had asked for or wanted, although the Sumerian language continued to be used as a written language for a long time.

With this type of resentment simmering, Sargon needed to take steps to protect himself and legitimize his rulership. He created the first known class of soldiers called *niskum*, a group comparable to royal guards. To ensure their loyalty, these were also given generous perks, such as land and allotments of salt and fish— things that were very valuable in ancient times. These perks were effective in the case of the soldiers as well. It was so effective that Sargon's model for loyal professional soldiers was later used by Egyptian pharaohs and Roman emperors.

Once Sargon had loyal vassal rulers in place and a trusted royal military, he still needed something to further cement himself into his new position—something that could not quickly shake him out of it: the divine approval of his kingship. Despite the differences in language and culture between the Sumerians and Akkadians, one thing they could essentially agree on was religion. So, by mixing his rule with religion, he could theoretically create a more seamless transition for his dynasty.

He started to put on this "mantle" of legitimacy right from the start. In Kish, he was a usurper, so if the patron deity of the city was not behind him, no one else would likely be either. This would be tricky considering that the patron god of Kish was none other than Zababa—a minor god from which the deposed Ur-Zababa (literally meaning "man of Zababa") had wisely derived his name. Sargon needed a way to draw a line from himself to Zababa, and he managed this by identifying his personal god, Ilaba, with Zababa. Once he had established that the patron deity was behind him, it was hard for anyone to question the legitimacy of his rule. He had turned himself from usurper to an agent of the gods.

But as Sargon's empire grew, being associated with a minor local deity wasn't going to cut it anymore. The bigger the empire, the bigger the deities backing him needed to be. He eventually dropped his identification with Zababa and went straight to the top, connecting himself to the supreme deities of the Sumerian/Akkadian pantheon, Enlil and Ishtar (the Akkadian counterpart of the Sumerian goddess Inanna).

He took another leap further in connecting his kingship to the priesthood by installing his daughter Enheduanna in Ur as the high priestess of the moon god Nanna.[29] It would be close to the equivalent of giving your daughter in a marriage alliance with a deity and setting her up in a mansion dedicated to the god. After all, the temple in Ur was only second to the temple of Eanna in Nippur. This move was also a way to retain control over the priesthood while looking extremely important and increasing his appeal among the people, especially those in such an important city as Ur. He also made sure to honor people of other cities by paying tribute to every local deity he came across—a move that surely appeased many hearts and won him points.

If that wasn't enough, Sargon went even further, just to make sure everyone knew the gods protected him as the legitimate ruler. He began widely using the images of lions everywhere, from statues guarding the palace to axes with blades that looked like they were coming out of a lion's mouth to lions carved on the hilts of daggers. The images of these fierce beasts were not just used for intimidation purposes; they were signs of power, kingship, and protection. They were also the symbol of the goddess Ishtar, further tightening Sargon's connection with the supreme beings.

---

[29] Enheduanna was one of Sargon's five children by Queen Tashlultum. Other than a single shard of alabaster pottery with a brief inscription of her name, there is no other mention of Sargon's wife in known archaeology. It is assumed that she was a queen and that Sargon's other children—Rimush, Manishtushu, Shu-Enlil, and Ilaba'is-takal—were hers as well.

Akkadian ax head with lion carving.

It was much easier to phase out an entire political and cultural identity when the people thought it was the will of the gods. But though Sargon was slowly wiping away traces of Sumerian culture and systems and replacing it with Akkadian ones, the Sumerians did not forget that their once-great culture existed. As can be imagined, many of them did not take too kindly to suddenly becoming foreigners in their own cities.

However, no matter how good Sargon had been or how well he had implemented this plan, boiling resentment created cracks in the foundation that held the empire together. The dam of revolt eventually broke near the end of his reign.

The "elders of the land," those whose authority he had removed early on, finally pulled together a rebellion. Later Babylonian chronicles state that "In his old age, all the lands revolted against him, and they besieged Akkad. But Sargon went forth to battle and defeated them; he knocked them over and destroyed their vast army.

Later, Subartu in their might attacked, but they submitted to his arms and Sargon settled their habitations, and he smote them grievously."

Sargon was likely more than seventy years old when he rode out to personally oversee the rebellion-crushing campaign. In one of a series of revolts, the deposed authorities of Kish barricaded themselves in the temple of Inanna at Kish in protest. Sargon naturally claims to have quashed the revolt immediately.

Other revolts, though, may not have been put down so quickly or easily. Later Babylonian chronicles paint a completely different picture of what happened. In at least one battle against the revolutionaries, Sargon's forces did not find it easy to crush the opposers. Sargon was forced to jump into a ditch and hide as the rebels marched past him.[30]

In the year 2279 BCE, the fight was over for Sargon, who reportedly died of natural causes. But the death of the king did nothing to quell the rebellions that raged. They would be passed to the next ruler, his son, Rimush.

---

[30] It is obvious that accounts were slanted according to the biases of the tellers. Sargon naturally would write that he quickly put down rebellions, and anti-Sargon Akkadians would throw out propaganda that portrayed him as an old man cowering in a ditch. The truth probably lies somewhere in the middle.

Chapter 4 – Enheduanna

She may not have been as flashy, powerful, or jewel-laden as Queen Puabi, but Enheduanna, Sargon's daughter, certainly played a pivotal role in her father's empire. As mentioned before, without her, he may have had an even harder time holding on to his empire. But what do we know about her?

Her beginnings are somewhat of a mystery. There is no information about when or where she was born, and there is not even a record of who her mother or siblings were (other than the two royal brothers who succeeded Sargon the Great). Even her name, which means "priestess fit for heaven," is unlikely the name she was given after birth; she likely took it only after she became a high priestess.[31]

With no previous religious training necessary, her father shot her straight to the top of the priesthood, installing her as high priestess of the moon god Nanna, one of the most prominent deities of the Akkadian pantheon.[32] The promotion was a political strategy rather

---

[31] It was common for ancient people to change their names or have them changed by others based on dominant personality traits, professions, or other things that identified that person.

[32] During Enheduanna's time, priests managed the temples. Common citizens did not go there to worship—the priests and priestesses worshiped them there on behalf of the people.

than a burning desire for his children to serve the gods. There is no telling whether she wanted or inwardly agreed with the move, but it's unlikely she had any choice. If there was any reluctance on her part, it was compensated with immense prestige. The high priestess of Nanna was viewed as the representation of his wife Ningal, and she would be imbued with divine authority and given honor nearly as great as the king himself.

In addition, she could have the satisfaction of knowing that she was proving to the people her father's piety, honor, and submission to the deities. Without this grand display, Sargon could not have connected his new Akkadian dynasty with the deep religious roots of the Sumerian people.

Ruins of the temple complex where Enheduanna served (front).

Disk picturing Enheduanna dressed as a high priestess with a nude male figure pouring out a drink, perhaps as an offering to Nanna.

Beyond the scene depicted on a disk found among the temple ruins, which depicted a nude man pouring out a drink (perhaps as an offering to Nanna), not much is known about Enheduanna's exact duties as a high priestess. She likely oversaw rituals, oversaw the temple complex, and may have even acted as her father's representative in the city.

Next to the royal family, the priests of a temple were the most important, honored, and prestigious people of the city. They were not shut up in monk-like seclusion in the temples, but they took care of the fertile grounds allotted to the temple, distributed the food grown there, and collected taxes, among other more secular functions. Priestesses usually did not have as much power as the priests, but Enheduanna had one thing going for her that no other high priestess in history had—her father was the emperor. Since the power of the king and the city's priests were in a connected sort of symbiotic relationship, it was unlikely that Enheduanna was looked down on or took orders from the priests. She likely had the final word in the temple. The temples possessed a lot of wealth, so having his daughter in charge of one of the most prominent temples was much to Sargon's advantage. This kind of nepotism was sure to have made waves and created controversy.[33]

Though she appears to have been the first royal daughter to be set up in such a prominent position, there is something else that made Enheduanna special and set her apart from other women and even men. She was a poet and songwriter, and she is the earliest known named author in all of world history.[34] Her works predate the writing of some of history's oldest literature, including Homer's *Odyssey* and the Hebrew (Old Testament) books of the Bible by over one thousand years.

Just the fact that she was a known author of her time tells us two things about Enheduanna. She was literate (something common for royal women and high priestesses of the time). Her support from her royal father, along with her high status, also allowed her to include herself in her poems and hymns. She even wrote in first person in some instances.[35] But we learn so much more from her writings—we get a glimpse into who she was, the religious culture she centered her life around, and even references to historical events that are not found anywhere else.

Although she was a high priestess of Nanna, Enheduanna's poems and songs indicate that she had a very strong connection with the goddess Inanna, who was the subject of many of her works.[36] Through poetic language, she creates a picture of how she and the people

---

[33] Some scholars, such as Benjamin Foster, believe that Enheduanna's appointment was a "heavy-handed" move, forcing the integration of the Akkadian and Sumerian pantheon of deities. Sargon's move to appoint his daughter to such an important position may have had the opposite effect Sargon had intended. Instead of connecting himself to the Sumerians, some likely resented this move.

[34] Yale scholar and professor of Assyriology and Babylonian literature William Wolfgang Hallo dubbed her the "Shakespeare of Sumerian Literature."

[35] Some scholars suggest that of the forty-seven poems and hymns attributed to Enheduanna, she may actually have written very few or even none of them herself. But the fact that some of them are written in the first person lends credence to her being the author.

viewed Inanna, the goddess of love and war. She paints a picture of a deity who displays both cruelty and kindness, of someone who is loving and at the same time cruel—very similar to the complexities of human nature.

In her poem, "Exaltation of Inanna," Enheduanna talks about herself.[37] She appears to have had a healthy self-image, projecting one of beauty, talent, and strength. We see this in the lines of the poem where she speaks about her "mellifluous [sic] mouth" and mourning that the "choicest features [of her body] are turned to dust."[38]

She had confidence in her position, proclaiming, "I, the high priestess, I Enheduanna! / I am the brilliant high priestess of Nanna."

She also lets us know that she took serious care of her responsibilities as the high priestess. "I carried the ritual basket, I chanted your praise." And in her poem "Lady of the Largest Heart," she tells us how she advanced the worship of Inanna, saying, "I who spread over the land/the splendid brilliance/of your divinity."

But like any person, she experienced grief, begging, "Let me give free vent to my tears." It appears in "Lady of the Largest Heart" that she may have come down with some sort of illness or disease, which she attributed to punishment for offending Inanna. "You allow my flesh/to know your scourging/my sorrow and bitter trial/strike my eye as treachery."

Her greatest grief, however, is described in the "Exaltation of Inanna." She describes what happened during a revolt by a Sumerian rebel named Lugal-ann. He came from the city of Uruk, and he overthrew Ur. Enheduanna was either forced to flee or was forcibly removed from her role as priestess. Her heartache can be felt in her own words:

---

[36] Her father, Sargon, was deeply devoted to the goddess, so it is not a great surprise that his daughter would follow suit.

[37] Though the following lines of the poem are accurate, their order has been mixed in order to tell the story in a more logical and understandable way.

[38] Mellifluous means having a sweet-sounding or musical voice.

"Me who once sat triumphant, he has driven out of the sanctuary.

Like a swallow he made me fly from the window,

My life is consumed

He made me walk through the thorns on the mountains

He stripped me of the crown appropriate for the high priesthood.

He gave me dagger and sword—'It becomes you,' he said to me.

It was in your service that I first entered the holy temple,

Now I have been cast out to the place of lepers.

Day comes and the brightness is hidden around me.

Shadows cover the light, drape it in sandstorms."

Enheduanna is not only grief-stricken for herself but is outraged at the audacity Lugal-ann has in desecrating Eanna, one of the greatest temples in ancient times. Not only that, but he goes as far as to set himself up in a high position and make sexual advances on his sister-in-law, the new high priestess. As Enheduanna tells it,

"[Lugal-ann] has altered the lustrations of holy An and all his [other rites].

He has stripped An of [his temple] Eanna.

He has not stood in awe of An-lugal

That sanctuary whose attractions are irresistible, whose beauty is endless,

That sanctuary he has verily brought to destruction.

Having entered before you as a partner, he has even approached his sister-in-law."

Enheduanna watched as her city and its temples were destroyed by a man who appeared to once be an ally, one who was apparently personally known to her. She called to the gods to save the city from the treachery of Lugal-ann:

"[Uruk] is a malevolent rebel against your Nanna—may An make it surrender!

This city—may it be sundered by An!

May it be cursed by Enlil!

May its plaintive child not be placated by his mother!

Oh lady, the [harp of] mourning is placed on the ground.

One had verily beached your ship of mourning on a hostile shore.

At [the sound of] my sacred song they are ready to die.'

Enheduanna receives no answer from Nanna, and she is pretty bitter about his lack of protection. She laments, "As for me, my Nanna takes no heed of me." She's done the only thing she can do to help save the city, and when that fails, she feels utterly powerless, crying out,

"He has verily given me over to destruction in murderous straits.

Ashimbabbar[39] has not pronounced my judgment.

Had he pronounced it: what is it to me? Had he not pronounced it: what is it to me?"

At some point, Enheduanna is removed from her position and exiled. In the desperation of the situation, Enheduanna calls on Inanna to plead with the powerful sky god An on her behalf and avenge her.[40]

"Say thus to An: 'May An release me!'

Say but to An 'Now!' and An will release me.

This woman will carry off the manhood of Lugal-ann.

That woman is as exalted—she will make the city divorce him.

Surely she will assuage her heartfelt rage for me.

Let me, Enheduanna, recite a prayer to her...

---

[39] Another name for Nanna.
[40] An is the Akkadian Anu.

Oh my queen beloved of An, may your heart take pity on me!"

She also appeals to Inanna on behalf of Nanna, the goddess's husband, and appeals to Inanna as a child pleading with her mother, saying,

"[Only] on account of your captive spouse, on account of your captive child,

Your rage is increased, your heart unassuaged."

Enheduanna depicts Inanna as a warlike storm bird—fearsome, battle-ready, and powerful. She puts her confidence in Inanna's warrior abilities and asks her to haunt and take vengeance on Lugalann, calling out,

"Oh my lady, [propelled] on your own wings, you peck away [at the land].

In the guise of a charging storm you charge.

With a roaring storm you roar.

With Thunder you continually thunder.

With all the evil winds you snort.

Your feet are filled with restlessness...

Like a dragon you have deposited venom on the land.

When you roar at the Earth like thunder, no vegetation can stand up to you...

Devastatrix of the lands, you are lent wings by the storm."

Eventually, the crisis in Ur ended, and Enheduanna returned to the city and was restored to her position as high priestess. She credits Inanna with the victory, then praises and extols her beauty.

"The first lady, the reliance of the throne room,

Has accepted her offerings

Inanna's heart has been restored.

The day was favorable for her, she was clothed sumptuously, she was garbed in womanly beauty.

Like the light of the rising moon, how she was sumptuously attired!

...

[To] my lady wrapped in beauty, [to] Inanna!"

The revolt in Ur, as written by Enheduanna, likely happened during the reign of her nephew, Naram-sin. The Sumerians temporarily wrested power away from the Akkadians in Ur and other southern cities. It is not mentioned over what period of time the events in the poem happened, but eventually, Akkadian power was at least partially restored to the region. Enheduanna returned and resumed her position as high priestess, a position she held for more than forty years. During that time, she wrote numerous poems and hymns, many of which have been damaged over time, leaving us only pieces of her works. The "Exaltation of Inanna" is to date the longest and most complete work of Enheduanna's to be found.

Even years after her death, Enheduanna remained an important figure—perhaps even reaching semi-divine status. Her role as a princess and high priestess set a precedent for royalty for many centuries and cultures. Over the next five hundred years of Sumerian history, royal families installed their daughters as high priestesses in Ur, linking royalty and divinity together. It was a move that acknowledged Sargon's political savvy. Aside from being considered masterpieces of ancient literature, Enheduanna's writings were used as a sort of workbook to teach subsequent priests, priestesses, and even scribes how to write.

In the modern day, Enheduanna is remembered as a poet priestess whose numerous works give us a firsthand glimpse into a life that not much had been written about. It is also a rare personal account of the life of a woman in ancient times. Most of the writings in ancient history were done by and about men.

Enheduanna was not the only one of her father's royal children to enjoy both a high position and hard times. Her brothers succeeded Sargon, but their stories did not end as well as hers.

Chapter 5 – The Sons of Sargon

Head of a Mesopotamian ruler, possibly Rimush.

Sargon's son Rimush gained a large inheritance upon his father's death. But aside from the crown of a king, he also inherited an empire burning with revolt. His father had managed to unify the city-states, but the union was tenuous at best. Revolution had already begun to take hold at the end of Sargon's life, but a change on the throne did nothing to quell the rebellions and chaos. In fact, it may have fanned the flames.

By all rights, Rimush should not have inherited the throne in 2279 BCE; it should have gone to his older brother, Manishtushu, Sargon's oldest son. For reasons that remain a mystery,[41] Rimush, the second son,[42] took over his father's empire.

Whereas Sargon used language, religious connections, trade routes, and postal services to try to keep the empire united, Rimush laid down a heavy hand on those who rebelled. He would be known for keeping the empire intact through extreme force and cruelty.

There was no easy transition into the kingship for Rimush; he didn't get a chance to slide in and adjust to the throne. Rather, he was baptized by fire. Some revolts questioned the very legitimacy of his rule. But whatever the cause, the cities that rebelled would soon learn that he was no weakling to be trifled with.

And it wasn't just a few outliers that Rimush had to contend with. Most of the major cities of the empire rose up in rebellion, including Lagash, Umma, and Ur. By his own accounts, his retribution against them came swiftly and decisively.

With brutal force, he tore down the walls of the cities and dealt ruthlessly with their inhabitants. Thousands of rebel soldiers were killed, but non-combatants did not fare much better, as many ordinary citizens were likely casualties of war. Men of fighting age were taken from the city. Many were sold as slaves, and others were sent to live a hard life in what were possibly labor camps.

A massive seizure and transfer of lands followed. In what was one of the biggest land transactions in all of ancient history, 321,237 acres of farmland were taken from rebellious landowners around Lagash and Umma—lands for which they had fought hard over for many

---

[41] His father may have seen something in him that prompted him to make his second son the successor to the throne—perhaps a ruthless decisiveness that was required to hold together an empire that was about to come apart. Or it may have been that Rimush actually was the stronger brother and took the throne himself after Sargon's death.

[42] Some historians speculate that the brothers may have actually been twins.

years—and promptly awarded them to the land-owning Akkadians who supported the empire. The Akkadian conquerors also demoted the Sumerian priests—men and women believed to be assigned to their positions by the gods—and installed Akkadians in the temples instead, a practice that was a continuation of what Sargon had started.

In a departure from centuries of Sumerian tradition, a culture of nepotism now prevailed. Those who benefited from it were all too happy to drop the old traditions to enrich and promote themselves and their families. But it surely angered a lot of people, like the priests and Sumerian elites who lost ancestral lands their families had held for centuries. The disregard the Akkadians had for the Sumerian traditions did nothing to quell the rebellious spirit among the Sumerians.

Despite the swiftness of Rimush's rebellion-crushing crusade, other cities either did not learn from those that fell or were not intimidated by Rimush's forces. The fires of revolt continued to spring up and rage. For example, the city of Kazallu fared no better than the rest.

The city had previously rebelled against Sargon, and it did not turn out well—many of its citizens were butchered in an effort to put down the uprising. Now they would try their hand against the son. But when Rimush's forces came up against the city, they found out the hard way that they would fare no better against this king. Rimush savagely put down the resistance, killing not only around twelve thousand soldiers but many non-combatants as well. Five thousand citizens were sold into slavery, and like his father, he tore down the walls of the city.[43]

Rimush didn't just stop at the rebels of Sumer. After having solidified his position in the empire, he also went on to campaign against the independent neighboring kingdoms of Elam (part of

---

[43] In general, the walls of the cities were not entirely torn down, but there were either significant breaches or the gates were torn off, rendering them indefensible. So, the fact that the people rebelled against Sargon and continued to rebel against Rimush, despite having cities that were vulnerable to the king's forces, showed how much hatred the Sumerians had for their Akkadian conquerors.

modern-day Iran). He crushed and defeated the cities of that mountainous region as well, with the body count piling up across the region. An inscription claimed that after his victory in Elam, Rimush brought an immense amount of wealth back to Akkad and Nippur. It is believed he had captured thousands of pounds (minas) of copper and gold, as well as hundreds of slaves. The king of Elam and his nobles were among the captives.

A depiction of a captive of Rimush's forces, bound by the wrist and led by a ring through the nose.

Rimush was not shy about extolling his victories. He took meticulous records of his destruction, including numbers of the slain, captives, and those expelled from the cities. However, he did dedicate some of the spoils of war to the temple of Enlil, the god who he credited with his victories, saying, "Rimush, king of the entire world: the god Enlil gave to him all the land."

He also made sure to dedicate something important to himself—a large lead statue of his likeness. Lead might not be a big deal or even considered precious in modern times, but in ancient times, it was a precious rarity. A tablet from the period makes this clear, as it reads, "From the earliest days no one had made a statue of lead, but Rimush, king of Kish, had a statue of himself made of lead." That would be the equivalent of someone making a statue of themselves out of diamonds today. Rimush wanted to impress the people and project an image of immense wealth and power. He wanted to be seen essentially as an immortal figure. Intoxicated with his own success, he imaged himself more of a god than a mere human. In the end, however, he proved to be just as mortal as everyone else.

Rimush's nine years of rule were awash in blood and battle, but he did manage to hold the empire together for the most part. But in 2271 BCE, he died suddenly. The evidence points to assassins in his own court. Sources indicate that his court officials bashed him over the head or strangled him with their seals—an ignominious death for someone who viewed themselves as having god-like power. No one knows for sure who the mastermind was behind his death; the man had no shortage of enemies. But there was one person who stood to gain the most from his death—his brother, Manishtushu.

Manishtushu's reign started no better than his brother's, as he was also baptized in the fire of quelling rebellions. But unlike his brother, it would not be the defining trait of his reign.

After the rebellions were stamped out, Manishtushu sought to expand his empire, and this would have to be done largely through a show of force. A prime example of that was when Manishtushu took his naval fleet down the Persian Gulf to the area now known as the United Arab Emirates and Oman. Once he arrived, he was not greeted with a warm welcome. Instead, thirty-two kings had allied to fight him, and he was welcomed with their armies. Despite what seemed like overwhelming odds, Manishtushu proved victorious. He took treasures from the region's silver mines, and he was in a prime position to invade other kingdoms. Records indicate he may have gone as far as the Indus Valley in his quest to expand his empire.

When he wasn't busy defeating multitudes of allied kings and acquiring new lands, Manishtushu was somewhat of a shrewd wheeler and dealer. Besides establishing trade links with faraway places like Egypt, there was one event of interest that was recorded in picture form on clay tablets. In Akkad, 964 men were invited to a feast where they were plied with delicacies such as meat, bread, and olives. The beer flowed freely. But this was no ordinary feast. There was no joy or dancing, and the men eating may not have had much appetite given the circumstances. Those nearly one thousand men were there to give up their lands (probably involuntarily) in exchange for food—a mere two years' worth of harvests. The men charged with overseeing the feast and the exchange, possibly some of whom would receive the surrendered lands, oversaw the event to make sure there was no trouble from the disgruntled former landowners. It seemed to be a repeat of the same indignities that had sparked rebellions during the last two reigns—land taken from its owners and given to a new elite class of Akkadian cronies of the king.

The incident, along with others, was really a reflection of the attitudes the Akkadian kings had toward the Sumerians and their established institutions. Manishtushu, like his father and brother, had no problem treading over the people to expand their own power, wealth, and circle of influence.

Despite continuing the sins of his family members, his rule actually stabilized the empire far more than the warring reigns of the past. He managed to finish the rebellions started under Rimush's reign, but there are indications that Manishtushu was more inclined toward peace than war—well, relatively, at least compared to his father and brother. There are sculptures showing him trampling on his enemies, after all. But for the most part, an empire that had been in a near-constant state of war for many years was finding life a bit more settled.

A depiction of Manishtushu trampling his enemies underfoot.

Manishtushu did not forget to connect himself to religion and show his piety among the people, dedicating statues to the god Enlil and building a temple to Inanna (Ishtar) in Nineveh. He, of course, made sure to have statues and obelisks dedicated to himself as well.

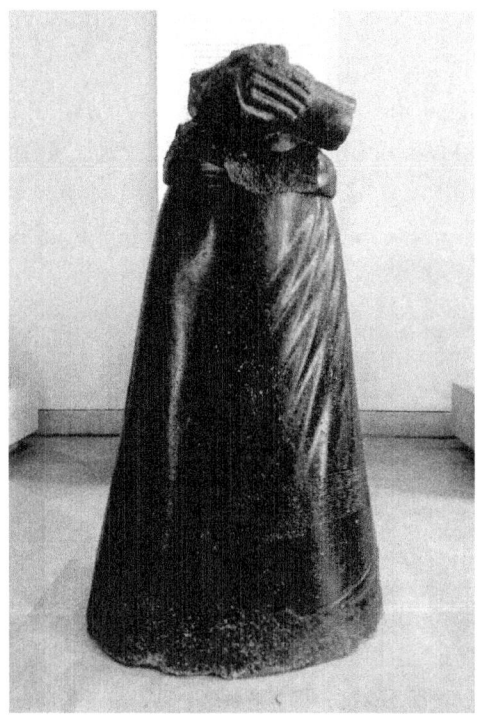

Statue of Manishtushu.

An obelisk from Manishtushu's reign.

Though the empire experienced a measure of peace during his reign, Manishtushu also managed to create a lot of enemies during his fifteen years on the throne, with some of those enemies being members of his own court.

In an eerie repeat of his brother's demise, it appears that in 2255 BCE, a court conspiracy ended with his assassination, though records of the details seem to be missing or nonexistent.

Whether it was plotted by people who simply hated him or if it was a usurpation instigated by his son, who had been waiting in the wings to take the throne, Manishtushu left his successor with an inheritance of rebellious city-states. Could his son, Naram-sin, turn the empire around?

Chapter 6 – Naram-sin Takes the Empire to Soaring Heights and Tragic Depths

Proud, arrogant, and warrior-like, Naram-sin ascended the throne with the same supreme confidence of his near-legendary grandfather, Sargon. But before he would reach his self-declared divine status, he would set his sights on expanding the empire and have his reign tested in the fire of rebellion. He took the throne and hit the ground running.

Ancient texts portray him as a terrifying conqueror with the aura and power of a wild animal, likening him to a raging lion. That may have been how the hill tribes to the north felt as he swept through, conquering regions from the northern Mediterranean and into the Zagros, Taurus, and Nur (Amanus) Mountains all the way up to modern-day Armenia.

Stele portraying the victory of Naram-sin over Satuni, King of Lullubi, in the mountainous region bordering modern-day Iraqi Kurdistan and Iran.

Naram-sin was supremely confident in his campaigns, whether they involved stamping out rebellions or gaining territory for the empire. Rebellions sprang up from the get-go, but the rebelling cities were unorganized and did not coordinate with each other, which was a huge mistake since they were taking on a fierce king with the blood of an empire-builder running through his veins. As entities standing alone against the king and their armies in disarray, they were no match for the empire's disciplined professional army, which easily put them down.

One of Naram-sin's most famous campaigns, the one against the Lullubi people of the eastern Iranian Zagros Mountains, was commemorated on a victory stele that depicts Naram-sin standing at the head of his army, triumphant over piles of his defeated enemies.[44]

However, he didn't give all the credit to his army or even himself. He claimed that he had some superhuman help along the way, saying that the gods went with him and opened the road for his army. He specifically mentions that he escorted Ishtar to her battle and that she went with him as a companion, bringing a "hostile fury" whose "battle overwhelmed the land." He also claimed that the god Assur put an "unsparing scimitar into his hand to overthrow his enemies."

Naram-sin exalted over his relatively minor victories over these poorly trained hill armies and tamping down small rebellions. But he would soon face an event that would shake his empire to its core. It was nearly an empire-ending war, aptly dubbed the "Great Revolt," one in which he claimed the four corners of the world came up against him.[45]

Although the claim is dramatized and hyperbolic, the northern and southern parts of the empire did, in fact, rise up against him. Naram-sin had to fight a number of battles nearly back-to-back in order to preserve his kingdom.

In the north, Iphur-Kish, King of Kish, came to power but in a very unusual way for ancient Mesopotamia. He was *chosen* to be king by the citizens of his city-state. Democracy was not a thing back then—it was basically unheard of. When Naram-sin found out about this abomination against inherited or "divinely appointed" kingship, he angrily called Iphur-Kish a pretender to the throne. His kingship was an affront to the gods and the kings they actually appointed. In reality, it wasn't so much that a king had been chosen or who it was, but Naram-sin knew this action was bad news for his own kingship, potentially putting it in a precarious position by setting a dangerous

---

[44] Popular history connects horned helmets with the Vikings, but as the victory stele shows, the Akkadians wore them first!

[45] The main literary work written regarding the event is the ancient writing called "The Great Revolt."

precedent. If the people of Kish could choose their own king, what was to say others wouldn't follow?

The resulting rebellion that the new king of Kish put together really tipped the scales.[46] Iphur-Kish had learned his lesson from the disorganized and uncoordinated rebellions that had occurred before. He created a coalition, and he brought in the metaphorical big guns—large cities such as Kazallu, Sippar, Cutha (Kutha), and others. They allied themselves to fight against Naram-sin and Agade (Akkad).

Naram-sin claimed that he treated Kish as an ally. In the surviving texts from the time, he shows an obvious bias in his own version of events. Naram-sin contrasts his innocent goodness with the evil treachery of Kish, which repaid his good with evil.

Accounts tell that Naram-sin shut the gates of Agade and made an impassioned speech to the god Shamash before the people, perhaps reminding the deity how he had given the Kishites royal grace, and now they were showing their ingratitude for all that had been done for them. After the speech, he rallied his army to battle. They marched out to meet the Kishites and their allies.

Although inscriptions mentioned the gods going with Naram-sin, nowhere does he claim they took any action on his behalf. In fact, inscriptions depict him as standing alone before the battlefield. Of course, his army of tens or hundreds of thousands was behind him, but he is seen as having no aide-de-camp or advisor that he could turn to for help. He courageously made all the decisions alone and led the army, hurling himself into battle along with his men against what he claimed were the superhuman forces of all the rebel cities lined up in battle formation.

---

[46] Sumerian tradition says that the revolt was started by Naram-sin's efforts to rebuild Ekur (also known as Duranki), a very important mountain top religious complex. It was basically the Mount Olympus of ancient Sumer. In 2300 BCE, his grandfather Sargon had destroyed the richly furnished, gold-laden Ekur, much to the lament of the people.

With his armies routed on the battlefield, Iphur-Kish retreated back to his city. But Naram-sin was not going to let him just get away and run home. He pursued Iphur-Kish to the city, where there was a second battle. The men fought in the streets of the city, with another 2,500 Kishites falling to Naram-sin's forces. He was again victorious. He said he filled the Euphrates River with the bodies of the slain. He also took many captives as slaves and trophies, with a number of them being distinguished or noble figures.[47]

But Naram-sin was still angry about the rebellion. Capturing the king and his city was not enough punishment for their evil deeds. He completely took down the city's walls and then diverted the Euphrates River to flow toward the city, completely flooding it. Only the complete obliteration of the city would be punishment enough.

Despite the devastation of the northern coalition, the Great Revolt did not end there. A southern coalition of cities appeared, and it seems it did not learn from the devastation wrought on their fellow rebels in the north. This southern coalition consisted of the cities of Adab, Nippur, Girsu, Isin, Lagash, Umma, and other cities. It was headed by the king of Uruk, who was named Amar-girida.[48]

Naram-sin, no doubt feeling confident after his most recent victories, marched down to meet the southern city-states on their own turf. He claims that he went unarmed and did not wait for the battle to come to him. Instead, he and his army ran out to meet the enemy forces head-on. As the battle between Naram-sin's army and the southern alliance raged, Amar-girida realized that the southern coalition was losing. He put out a call to some of the far northern cities to join him, but those cities already knew what had happened to the northern alliance, and they didn't want any part of it. Fearing the wrath of the gods and of the king, they refused to join the battle.

---

[47] He bragged about this in inscriptions, gloating over their captures by listing their names.

Without help, Uruk fell. Amar-girida was taken captive, and Naram-sin's forces captured all the treasures in the city. The city then received the same punishment that befell Kish—the walls were taken down, and the city was flooded. This was the final nail in the southern coalition's coffin.

The original texts don't give much in the way of details of these battles; only the final results are known. Naram-sin and his army fought ten battles—all in one year. Some ancient sources say that eighteen kings fought against Naram-sin and that the emperor's armies took heavy casualties before turning things around and gaining victory. Late Akkadian sources portrayed Naram-sin's victories over the rebels as nothing short of miraculous. There was no way a mere mortal could have pulled it off—they surmised that he, therefore, must be divine. Well, that's at least how he had himself portrayed in the stelae and statues he built to brag about his greatness.

In an inscription on the Bassetki Statue, a sculpture Naram-sin had made after his victory and in which only the lower half of a bronze man remains, he laments and brags that he experienced something that no other king in history had ever been through before—the four corners of the earth, literally the "whole world," had come up against him. And he beat them. He says in the inscription, "Naram-sin, the mighty, king of Agade, when the four quarters of the earth attacked him together, through the love Ishtar bore him, he was victorious in nine battles in a single year and captured the kings whom they had raised up against him. Because he defended his city in crisis, the people of his city asked of him that he be a god of their city Agade with Ishtar in Eanna, with Enlil in Nippur, with Dagon in Tuttul, with Ninhursag in Kesh, with Enki in Eridu, with Sin in Ur, with Shamash in Sippar, with Nergal in Cutha, and they built his temple in Agade."

---

[48] Some sources name Lugal-ann as one of the kings of this coalition. It is possible that these events were connected to the events referred to in Enheduanna's poem, the "Exaltation of Inanna."

Not only did he set in bronze just how awesome he was in being able to defeat the whole world, but he also claimed that it proved the gods were with him. This would serve to let any other would-be rebels know that if they came up against him, they were also going up against heaven, making them think twice about rebelling.

The inscription also indicates that he was deified—raised to the level of a god—in Agade. However, he wanted to make sure that everyone knew that *he* wasn't the one who deified himself. He indicates that the people saw his greatness and how well he had protected him and that they begged him to be the patron deity of Agade. The people even build a temple in his honor. But this is a gutsy, not to mention hubris-inducing, move, no matter how much he claimed it was the doing of the people. Not even Sargon dared to make himself a god, no matter how great he thought himself. Sargon always gave credit for his victories to Inanna/Ishtar and other gods, never declaring that it was due to his own divine might. As will be shown in later literary works, Naram-sin's crossing of the line from mortal to divine came at a very high cost.

Although the Great Revolt was the thing that stands out the most about Naram-sin's reign, he did have other accomplishments. Becoming a god did not mean he neglected the gods of other cities. For instance, he built and restored the temples of patron gods. Given that he credited Inanna/Ishtar with his victories, he was particularly devoted to her, and the goddess received the most lavish gifts and a temple dedicated to her.

Naram-sin also occupied himself with very human affairs. After conquering parts of Elam early on, he ended up making a peace treaty with King Khita, who sealed the pact with the words, "The enemy of Naram-Sin is my enemy, the friend of Naram-Sin is my friend." The two kings further strengthened their alliance when Naram-sin married Khita's daughter. He had one daughter and three sons, one of whom would inherit his empire.

Despite the remarkable successes of his reign, in 2218 BCE, Naram-sin died in an unremarkable way. After ruling the empire for thirty-six years, he simply died of old age. However, the two literary works that would be written about him would become legendary.

Chapter 7 – Truths Wrapped in Fiction: "The Legend of Cutha" and "The Curse of Agade"

If "The Great Revolt" was written as history with a touch of fiction, we can say the reverse is true when it comes to the two famous legends that came from Naram-sin's era—"The Legend of Cutha" and "The Curse of Agade." Both are considered the empire's greatest examples of naru literature, a genre of writing that modern-day scholars dub as "fictional autobiography."[49] Though the basic historical facts are true, there is a lot of "creative storytelling" involved. However, the stories were not written simply as a way to change history; they were also an entertaining way to teach morals and lessons.

"The Legend of Cutha" reveals the necessity of obeying the gods and not relying on the wisdom of oneself, which many would agree is

---

[49] Naru is the Akkadian word for stele, many examples of which have been noted in previous chapters. On these stelae, kings bragged of their great deeds and victories. Though the foundation of what they told was true, they were not above using heavy embellishments and dramatic effect in the storytelling, often omitting defeats and generally anything that made the king look bad.

not an uncommon teaching.[50] However, in the poem, there is another interesting lesson, one that is not of morality or spirituality but posterity. It tells of the importance of leaving behind an account of one's life.

The poem starts out with very interesting and unusual, if not mysterious, lines:

"Open the tablet box and read the stele

That I, Naram-Sin, a descendant of Sargon

Inscribed and left behind for perpetuity."

The poem then dives straight into the lesson about leaving behind a record of one's life. However, the person that the lesson is about is not Naram-sin but Enmerkar, the first king and reputed founder of Uruk. After Naram-sin tells that he left his story to be read for eternity, he states that Enmerkar disappeared, perhaps in a metaphorical sense since he disappeared from history.

He goes on to say that even though Enmerkar was very pious—he had a good relationship with the gods—he, his ancestors, and his descendants ended up being severely punished by the gods. But what was Enmerkar's mistake? He apparently did not leave behind a record of his doings. This is a rather harsh punishment for someone who served the gods and, by all accounts, was a heroic warrior.

"The one whose wisdom and weapons bound, defeated, and killed those troops

Did not write on a stele, he did not leave one behind for me and

he did not make a name for himself and I did not pray for him."

Naram-sin claims that he was also affected by Enmerkar's mistake, blaming his omission for a tragic defeat and the entire devastation of Akkad. It's pretty obvious to see where the exaggerations come in. But the story goes even further than that. Naram-sin then tells of a race of

---

[50] "The Legend of Cutha" is also known by the title "Naram-sin and the Enemy Hordes."

people created by the gods. At first, he portrays them as abominations but then tells how they were turned into humans of extraordinary beauty,

"Their maternal goddess, Belet-ili, beautified them.

On the midst of the mountains they grew, they reached manhood,

They acquired their proper size.

Seven kings, brothers, renowned for beauty,

Their troops numbered 360,000."

Their army is large and fearsome, and they go out and conquer many lands and kings. Their victories are so epic that Naram-sin concludes that they must be superhuman.[51] But he's not sure, so he devises a test to find out.

"I summoned a soldier and gave him orders.

I handed over a dagger and a pin.

'Attack with the dagger, prick with the pin.

If blood comes out, they are human like us.

If blood does not come out, they are spirits, fiends from the underworld.'"

The soldier goes out to perform the test and comes back to report his findings. It turns out that they were human after all; their army was just *really* good. Naram-sin decides that since they are human, they can be defeated, and he will be the one to do it. He asks the gods about going to war, but they tell him no. Naram-sin, unsurprisingly, does not like that answer. He scoffs, saying that the answer must have been wrong because of some scheming or fault on the part of the

---

[51] The superhuman army is not identified in the poem as belonging to any particular race or region, but some scholars connect them with the Gutians because it matches with Sumerian texts that describe the Gutians as "an unbridled people, with human intelligence but with the instincts of dogs and the appearance of monkeys." However, this connection is unlikely given the fact that, in the poem, Naram-sin mentions Gutium being defeated by these people.

diviners who asked. He decides that it's best to do what he wants, despite the advice he was given.

"Thus I said to myself, thus indeed I spoke:

'What lion practiced divination?

What wolf inquired of an interpreter of dreams?

Let me go like a bandit, following the counsel of my own heart.

Let me disregard the counsel of the god; let me take responsibility for myself.'"

Naram-sin sends his tens of thousands of soldiers out to battle, not once but twice. The first time, 120,000 men were sent out, and not one of them lived. It would seem that after such an incredibly catastrophic battle, Naram-sin would back down. But his pride gets the better of him, and he sends out another ninety thousand soldiers. Not one man returned alive from either battle.

Naram-sin is extremely grieved for a number of reasons. The first reason is about how he will go down in history for this.

"I was disturbed, perplexed, anxious, distressed, and dejected.

Thus I said to myself, thus indeed I spoke:

'What have I left behind as the legacy of my reign?'"

But he also realizes that in his pride and arrogance, he has made a terrible mistake. He has let his people down as their ruler. This is more than just disappointment; his mistake has brought his people untold disaster. He doesn't know how to fix it.

"I am a king who has not looked after his land,

And a shepherd who has not looked after his people.

How can I keep proceeding? How can I save my country?

Dread of lions, death, fate, famine

dismay, chills, losses, hunger,

Starvation, insomnia—every sort of calamity descended upon them.

Above, in the assembly, the flood was devised."

Humbled by his disastrous decision, he makes sacrifices and promises to hereafter obey anything the gods tell him. Not long after that, his promise is put to the test. He captures twelve men of the "superhuman" army. Wanting to kill them, he asks the gods if it is all right. Again, they tell him no. One of the gods explains the men of the enemy army will face a far worse punishment for their evil—judgment at the hands of Enlil.

"In the future, Enlil will raise them up for evil.

They await the furious heart of Enlil.

The city of those soldiers will be demolished.

They will burn and besiege the dwelling places.

The city will pour out their blood."

This time, Naram-sin was wise enough to listen. He ends the poem by once again urging future kings to find and read his stele and learn from his mistakes.

"You maintain self-control, you keep yourself in check...

Curb your boldness, look out for yourself! ...

I made you a tablet box, I inscribed for you a stele.

In Kutha, in the Emeslam temple,

In the shrine of Nergal I left it behind for you.

Read this stele,

And heed the message of this stele!"

In conclusion, he tells them that if they heed his warning, they will prosper and be blessed.

The real Naram-sin never faced or was defeated by a superhuman army, but he was used as the main character in the story to show that even a great king could make a terrible mistake yet receive forgiveness. The moral is that whether king or commoner, anyone can do the same and should learn from his example.

At the end of the Cutha revolt, Naram-sin comes out looking pretty good, having had redemption and turning from his errant ways. However, in "The Curse of Agade," the story is not so kind to the king's memory. For every story of heroism and redemption, there is an alternate tale that tells a different story. In the case of "The Curse of Agade," there is no redemption, only disaster for Naram-sin and his city of Akkad.

The story starts out with an idyllic picture of Akkad and its king. After the god Enlil destroyed the city of Kish, Naram-sin was placed on the throne in Akkad. He is depicted as a shepherd of the people and a protective warrior-king. The city is filled with all sorts of riches—precious gems, metals, grains, food, drink, exotic animals—they had it all. The people of the city were joyous pretty much all of the time. They danced, played instruments, and celebrated. The city was so awesome that even the goddess Inanna made her home there. The people built her a temple and overwhelmed her with gifts. Life couldn't get any better.

Things, however, begin to take a terrible turn. Naram-sin, being a pious man, is building (or rebuilding) Ekur, the temple of Enlil in the city of Nippur. Suddenly, a frightful message comes from the temple, and the whole city is paralyzed with fear,

"But the statement coming from the E-kur was disquieting.

Because of Enlil,

all Agade was reduced to trembling."

In the legend, no real reason is given for Enlil's wrath, but some scholars, reading between the lines, suppose that Enlil may have been angered because Naram-sin did not ask permission before building his temple, which was basically considered his house. It might be surmised that Enlil was angry because he gave power to the king, but the king presumed to take on the building project without first asking Enlil, who was, of course, the real and supreme authority. Whatever the reason, Enlil's wrath is so fearsome that even Inanna thought it best to hightail it out of the city, leaving the people to fend for themselves.

"Terror befell Inanna in Ulmac.

She left the city, returning to her home.

Holy Inanna abandoned the sanctuary of Agade like someone abandoning the young women of her woman's domain.

Like a warrior hurrying to arms, she tore away the gift of battle and fight from the city and handed them over to the enemy."

Life in Agade went downhill after that. All the riches, wisdom, joy, and might of the city were taken away, and it began to wither. "Like a dying dragon, it dragged its head on the earth."

Naram-sin is then given a dream about the future of the city, and it is grim. When he wakes, he is so disturbed by it that he doesn't even tell anyone what he saw.

Naram-sin goes into mourning for seven years, hoping to appease Enlil and turn the fate of the city around. But it doesn't work, and the king thinks it's outrageous that he's had to be in mourning for such a long time without any results. He then tries to make sacrifices and prays to Enlil to change his mind, but again, he receives no answer.

Angry about what he feels is unjust and unwarranted treatment by Enlil—as far as he's concerned, he's done nothing wrong—Naram-sin takes matters into his own hands. He gathers his troops and goes to the unfinished temple of Enlil. If Enlil does not want him to build the temple, then fine; he will destroy it, and he does so with great gusto,

"Like a robber plundering the city, he set tall ladders against the temple.

To demolish E-kur as if it were a huge ship, to break up its soil like the soil of mountains where precious metals are mined,

to splinter it like the lapis lazuli mountain, to prostrate it, like a city inundated by Ickur.

Though the temple was not a mountain where cedars are felled, he had large axes cast, he had double-edged axes sharpened to be used against it.

He set spades against its roots and it sank as low as the foundation of the Land.

He put axes against its top, and the temple, like a dead soldier, bowed its neck before him, and all the foreign lands bowed their necks before him.

He ripped out its drainpipes, and all the rain went back to the heavens.

He tore off its upper lintel and the Land was deprived of its ornament."

He even goes as far as to have the bedchamber of the temple destroyed; this would have been the equivalent of ripping apart Enlil's private bedroom, a pretty daring affront. To make matters worse, Naram-sin took all the precious metals, jewels, and treasures of the temple, though he didn't remove the wealth that belonged to the city itself. He has the precious metals and gems given to the metalsmiths and jewelers to be repurposed, and everything else was shipped out of the city. Essentially, after desecrating Enlil's house, he had robbed the god of his treasures. This is an unheard-of and frightening act of sacrilege on the part of Naram-sin.

Unsurprisingly, Enlil is extremely enraged by the insulting destruction and plunder of his house.[52] He is going to make Naram-sin pay for this, and he thinks about how he is going to punish the city for this outrageous treatment.

The other gods back him up. So now Naram-sin not only faces the wrath of Enlil but of the other gods as well. They send the Gutians, a

---

[52] Ancient Mesopotamians believed that the temples were the actual, physical homes of the gods. So, to them, destroying the temple was not a metaphorical destruction of the house of a god but a literal destruction of it.

people that are described as having animalistic features, to devastate the city.

"Enlil brought out of the mountains those who do not resemble other people,

who are not reckoned as part of the Land,

the Gutians, an unbridled people,

with human intelligence but canine instincts and monkeys' features."

The invasion causes great tragedy and desolation to the city. Food is hard to come by, and inflation is so out of control that it is difficult to buy even basic food products like oil. It is so bad that the city could not even bury their dead. Wild animals and violent men run rampant throughout the city. No one in the city can escape the terrible disaster that had befallen it.

"People were flailing at themselves from hunger...

Dogs were packed together in the silent streets; if

two men walked there they would be devoured by them,

and if three men walked there they would be devoured by them.

Noses were punched, heads were smashed, noses [?] were piled up, heads were sown like seeds.

Honest people were confounded with traitors, heroes lay dead on top of heroes, the blood of traitors ran upon the blood of honest men."

The city, with its gates ripped off and flung in the mud, becomes a place of overgrown desolation, lamentation, and sorrow. There is no happy ending, only praise by the gods for its destruction. The final line of the poem is "Inanna be praised for the destruction of Agade!"

Nowhere in history is there anything to suggest that the legend had much basis on facts. Naram-sin was quite diligent in worshiping the gods. While he did try to rebuild Ekur, there is no record of him tearing it down.

"The Curse of Agade" was written by an unknown author in an unknown year, probably after Naram-sin's reign. Likely by the time of its writing, fact and fiction had begun to be distorted. Some later works seem to tend toward promoting anti-Naram-sin propaganda, portraying Sargon as wise, heroic, and strong. In contrast, Naram-sin is painted as arrogant, impudent, and the bringer of disaster. In this case, there is a lesson to be learned. In short, don't overstep your bounds even if you are the king, and keep a good relationship with the gods, or else you are looking for trouble.

Besides lessons in morality and piety, these legends were also a way to engrave the main character into the minds of the people and keep their names known throughout history. We can see that it worked, given that these naru legends about Naram-sin are told even today. But there is a king who came before Naram-sin and Sargon, one whose epic tale has made indelible marks on history throughout the ages.

Chapter 8 – The Epic Gilgamesh

Just under four thousand years ago, the legend of a hero emerged—that of a king, his epic adventures, a quest for immortality, and redemption for tyranny. Said to be one-third mortal and two-thirds divine, King Gilgamesh of Uruk (also known as Erech) was an imposing figure. He was glorious, manly, and kingly in stature, so much so that even a goddess fell in love with him at first sight.

The *Epic of Gilgamesh* was originally an oral story, passed down through generations by word of mouth. It's unclear exactly when it started to be written down, but some historians believe that the Akkadians began to write it down during the height of their empire. The story is likely different from the original story as it was first told, as it would have changed to reflect the beliefs and values of the culture that wrote it.[53] The epic as we know it is decidedly Akkadian in its features.

---

[53] It was unlikely copied word for word from oral tradition, but the elements of the original story were added to it and changed to reflect the lessons and values that the Akkadians held as important.

Over time, the names of the gods and goddesses mentioned in the story changed as cultures shifted, but one name always remained the same—the hero of the story, King Gilgamesh.[54] This is his story.

One of the tablets of the Epic of Gilgamesh.

Gilgamesh's city of Uruk stood strong, with great inner and outer walls protecting the people inside. Grand temples to the chief god Anu and his daughter, the goddess of war and love, Inanna, stood out among the surrounding buildings. The king was proud when he surveyed all the grandeur he had built. But greatness caused the arrogant King Gilgamesh to become a tyrant to his people. He had absolute power, and he abused it terribly, crushing any and all who stood in his way.

The older men of the city are distressed by this. They go to him and tell him that a ruler should act more like a shepherd, guiding his

---

[54] Ancient records indicate that Gilgamesh was a real king of the city of Uruk (also known as the biblical Erech), but he ruled before the Akkadian Empire came into existence. However, the story was highly fictionalized by ancient writers.

people instead of coming up against them like a wild ox. They maintain that he is disgracefully arrogant and makes war just for his own amusement, which costs the people the lives of their sons. They tell him that he does not know or understand the plight of the people of his land, nor does he seem to care.

But proud Gilgamesh does not change his oppressive ways—he believes his kingship is from the gods and gives him the right to do whatever he wishes. The people of Uruk continue to complain among one another, and eventually, the sound of their complaints reaches the ears of the gods.

The gods turn to the goddess Aruru. She was the one who created Gilgamesh. The gods tell her that she needs to create another man who has the power to take down the tyrant. She takes some clay and spit and creates a man of the wild named Enkidu, who lives in the wilderness with the animals. One day, a hunter comes to a watering hole and sees this hairy wild man. Afraid, he runs back home. He tells his father that the wild man he saw was very powerful, perhaps the most powerful in the land, and that he disturbed his traps, ruining his ability to hunt.

The hunter and his father agree that the wild man is a problem and that they must find a way to get rid of him. They travel to Uruk and tell King Gilgamesh about the problem but also provide what they believe is the solution. They ask the king to send a prostitute to seduce Enkidu—and it works. He spends seven nights with her in the city, but afterward, he returns to the wilderness and his wild ways. However, the animals that he lived with senses something different about him, and they no longer accept him as their own. They run from him, and although he tries to chase them, he finds that he is weaker and can no longer run as fast as he could before.

Not knowing what else to do, he returns to the prostitute. She encourages him to be part of society, telling him about the delicious foods and fun festivals and all sorts of wonders he has never seen before.

But Enkidu is wild and unfit for civilization. He had spent so much time with the animals he almost became one. He has to be humanized first before he can be brought into society. So, the prostitute gives him his first set of clothes to wear. On the way to the city, they stop at a shepherds' camp. The shepherds give Enkidu beer, bread, and cooked foods—things he has never seen or heard of before. In the wild, he had lived on grass and animal milk. Thus, human foods are foreign to him, and at first, he eyes them cautiously. But he must learn how to eat and drink like a civilized human. The prostitute encourages him to eat, and when he does, he becomes a changed man. He sings, washes, and changes into clean clothes. Arming himself with a sword, he voluntarily goes out to watch over the shepherds' sheep during the night.

One day, a man comes into the camp carrying a beautiful ornamental dish. Decorative items are new to Enkidu, so the dish intrigues him. He asks the man where he is going, and the man tells him he is going to a wedding in Uruk. The man then tells Enkidu something that horrifies him. Although Gilgamesh is not the groom, he will abuse his power and institute the practice of *prima nocta*, which means he will be the first to sleep with the bride on the wedding night. This disgusts and infuriates Enkidu. He is determined to go to the city and challenge such an abusive tyrant.

But the prostitute tells Enkidu that Gilgamesh was lonely and wanted a friend. It turns out that Gilgamesh had two dreams about Enkidu prior to their battle. In the first, he saw a meteor land in a field outside the city. He used his great strength to lift the rock and gave it to his mother to take care of. In the second dream, Gilgamesh found an ax in the street and again took it to his mother. That time, his mother uncovered the meaning of the items he had found, telling him they symbolized a man who would come up against him but would turn out to be his most trusted friend. This friend would be one with the power to save and guide him.

Soon after, Enkidu is brought to Gilgamesh at Uruk. He goes into the city, angered by reports of Gilgamesh's tyrannical behavior, especially his treatment of women. His inherent sense of fairness has been offended, and Enkidu is eager to take the tyrant down a few pegs. Although Gilgamesh is reported to be very strong, Enkidu fully believes that Gilgamesh is no match for his wild power.

Once in the city, the people hail Enkidu as their champion for challenging the tyrant who has been oppressing them. He places himself in front of the bride's bedroom as a guard, and when Gilgamesh tries to enter, Enkidu blocks him. Gilgamesh then tries to force his way in, and the men become locked in an epic battle that spills into the streets.

The city shakes with the terrible rumbling of their battle. However, Enkidu realizes he has underestimated Gilgamesh's power. Eventually, the stronger Gilgamesh wrestles Enkidu to the ground, pinning him. Instead of finishing him off, both men find they have great respect for each other. The men forgive one another, and Enkidu acknowledges that Gilgamesh is indeed the superior fighter and he deserves to be king. Gilgamesh's mother declares that Enkidu is the very friend her son had dreamed about. From then on, the men become inseparable.

Feeling without purpose in life, Gilgamesh tells Enkidu he wants to team up for an adventure, but what kind of mission could they seek? Enkidu tells Gilgamesh about Humbaba, the tree monster of the faraway Cedar Forest, a place that the gods have banned humans from entering.

Gilgamesh is thrilled with the idea of this challenge, but Enkidu warns him that it will not be easy. Humbaba is invincible, and a mortal would be no match for him. Gilgamesh is undeterred. In fact, his desire for glory just motivates him even more. He says that even if he dies trying to battle the beast, he will still attain glory for his incredible courage. But if they do manage to kill the beast, their fame would be immortal. Also enticed by this idea, Enkidu agrees to go. However, if they are to slay the beast, they will need massive axes, swords, and bows, which they gather before their journey.

As they prepare to leave, they tell the people of Uruk about the grand adventure they are planning. They will not only slay Humbaba but also cut down the famed cedar trees that he protects. When the city elders hear about this, they are angered and horrified. They tell Gilgamesh that his quest is not only unwise but also outrageous. They also tell him that he arrogantly overestimates his own strength and foolishly underestimates the strength of Humbaba. Though the monster appears calm, his strength is great. But if he insists on going, he will not be able to do it alone. The journey through the vast wilderness requires the knowledge and expertise of Enkidu, the former man of the wild. The city elders also tell him that he better appeal to the sun god Shamash for protection as well.

So, before they go, Gilgamesh goes to his mother to gain her blessing. They also attend rituals of prayer and sacrifice made on their behalf in order to protect them on their journey.

The journey is very long—almost 450 miles. It would take normal men around three weeks to make the journey on foot, but the nearly superhuman power of Gilgamesh and Enkidu helps them to cover that distance in just three days. They reach the gates of the forest and gape in wonder as they look at the beauty of the surroundings. In the distance is an enormous mountain—the home of the gods.

It took them three days and nights to reach the mountain. During each of those three nights, Gilgamesh is plagued by terrifying dreams. In the first, a mountain fell on top of him. In the second, he was attacked by a wild bull while he could only lay helpless on the ground. But it was the third dream that scared Gilgamesh the most. In it, lightning and thunder shook the earth while fire and ash rained down from the sky. Enkidu interprets the dreams as signs of good fortune and protection from the gods, but the dreams have shaken Gilgamesh to his core. Afraid, he prays to Shamash for protection.

Shamash answers, telling Gilgamesh the reason he has had such terrifying dreams—it is Humbaba's doing. He explains that Humbaba's garment has seven layers, and each layer spreads fear. But fortunately, at that moment, the beast is only wearing one layer. If Gilgamesh is to go up against Humbaba, now is the perfect time. If he hesitates and Humbaba puts on all seven layers of his garment, he will be invincible, and Gilgamesh is sure to fail. He must strike now.

Gilgamesh and Enkidu continue until they reach the mountain of the gods they first saw from the gates of the forest. The mountain is forbidden to all humans, so in order to get Humbaba's attention and draw him down to them, they cut down some cedar trees.

Suddenly, Humbaba lets out a great and fierce roar as he realizes his trees have been felled. An infuriated Humbaba quickly appears to the men, and an intense battle ensues. Humbaba is stronger than the men had imagined, and the men fear they will lose the fight. When the fight becomes desperate for the humans, Gilgamesh calls out to Shamash for help. Shamash answers by sending thirteen storms. The storms stun Humbaba, giving Gilgamesh and Enkidu the chance to gain the upper hand while the beast is weakened.

Humbaba, knowing he is defeated, begs for mercy. He tells Gilgamesh that if he spares his life, he will become his servant. Gilgamesh considers this idea, but Enkidu insists that the beast must be slain. Angry at his harshness, Humbaba tells Enkidu he only wants him dead out of jealousy, for Enkidu fears that Humbaba will replace him as Gilgamesh's most trusted friend.

Humbaba then tries to put the fear of killing him into the men, saying that he is a servant of the supreme god Enlil, a god far greater and more powerful than Shamash. If the men were to kill Humbaba, Enlil would be sure to curse them. Enkidu refuses to be intimidated by the threats and urges Gilgamesh to quickly finish off the monster before Enlil can stop them. He knows they must slay Humbaba and steal his cedar trees if they are to achieve the glorious fame they came there to seek. The men quickly kill Humbaba and accomplish their quest.

They also find the tallest cedar in the forest and cut it down, making out of it a new gate for the city of Uruk. They then build two rafts in order to float back to the city with the gate and Humbaba's head as their trophies.

When the men return to the city, they clean themselves of the dirt and blood from their adventure. When Gilgamesh puts on new robes and steps out of the palace, the goddess of love, Inanna (Ishtar), sees him and is immediately struck by his handsomeness and his manly, muscular figure. She instantly falls in love, something that has never happened to her before.

She approaches Gilgamesh and begs him to marry her, promising that if he does, she will give him anything and everything he desires. But Gilgamesh is wary of her proposal. He tells her that since he has nothing a goddess could possibly need or want, her sudden love for him must really be only a shallow lust. He knows what has befallen her past lovers. When she tires of him, what will become of him? Will she send him to the underworld to cruelly torture him or turn him into an animal as she did to others? How could he expect to experience a better fate than those men?

Inanna is extremely offended and angered by Gilgamesh's rejection and the things he says about her. She goes up to her father and mother in heaven and asks for her brother-in-law, the Bull of Heaven (the constellation Taurus), to be sent down to exact revenge on Gilgamesh on her behalf. She wants to see the bull tear him apart for offending her so greatly. Her parents tell her that they do not understand why she is so angry because everything that Gilgamesh said about her is true. This only angers her even more. She tells them if she doesn't get what she wants, she will let out a tremendous scream that will cause the dead to rise from the netherworld and that once they are out, they will eat the living.

However, her father, Anu, still hesitates to give in to her wish, knowing that the bull will bring about a great calamity in the city—seven years of famine. But Inanna already knows that and has prepared for it, storing enough supplies for the city to get through the famine. Because of her prudent preparations and because her father doesn't want what amounts to zombies rising up and eating the living, he gives her what she wants.

The bull is sent down to Uruk, and when he falls from the sky and hits the ground, the great quake does incredible damage to the city. The earth itself cracks open and swallows up one hundred men. The bull gets up and lets out a fear-inspiring roar, the sound of which opens up more cracks in the earth. Another one hundred men fall into the openings and die. But the bull is not done venting his fury. The bull roars and opens the earth a third time.

After this third time, Gilgamesh and Enkidu spring into action to save the city. They battle the bull, but it has incredible power, so they need to work together and outsmart it. At the opportune moment, Enkidu takes the bull by its tail and holds it down. It gives Gilgamesh the chance to take his sword to slay the bull and cut out its heart, which he then sacrifices to Shamash.

A depiction of Gilgamesh and Enkidu killing the Bull of Heaven.

Inanna is furious that the men have slain the one she sent to avenge her honor. She climbs to the top of the city wall and hurls curses and insults at Enkidu and Gilgamesh. Unintimidated by her fury, they cut off a leg of the bull and throw it at her, telling her if she dares to come near them, they will do the same to her. Inanna mourns the bull while Gilgamesh and Enkidu cut off its head and ride around the city in victory before going back to the palace to enjoy a celebratory feast.

But the men fail to see that yet again, they have slain one who belongs to the gods. Though the gods seem to have overlooked the business with Humbaba, they won't turn a blind eye this time. The men have now defeated two supernatural beasts, and their deeds will not go without severe consequences.

That night, Enkidu has a nightmare that disturbs him greatly. In it, he sees the gods hold a meeting to discuss what happened. The gods agree that both men have gone too far in what they did—not only killing Humbaba and the bull but also daring to cut down the sacred cedar trees to make a gate. They decide that, in recompense, one of the men must die. The gods choose Enkidu as the one who will perish.

Enkidu soon falls ill, and he despairs so much that his sanity begins to falter. He rages and curses the cedar trees they cut down, the hunter who found him in the wilderness, and the prostitute who brought him to civilization, ruining his relationship with the animals and eventually leading him to Gilgamesh and his untimely death.

Shamash hears Enkidu's angry words and chides him for his rants by telling him that without those people, he would never have worn real clothes, tasted fine foods, or met his greatest friend. And further, it is Gilgamesh who will continue to suffer, walking the earth alone and filled with grief after Enkidu dies.

Enkidu continues to suffer for twelve more days. Like a madman, he dreams of the netherworld to which he is going. Gilgamesh tries to comfort Enkidu the only way he knows how, telling his friend that he will immortalize him and give him the fame he deserves by crafting an immense gold statue of him after he dies.

As Enkidu's death nears, Gilgamesh becomes hysterical and begs the gods to spare Enkidu, but his pleas are met with refusal. After the twelve days, Enkidu dies, and Gilgamesh is shattered with grief. However, he stays true to his promise and has the statue of Enkidu built. Enkidu is given an epic royal funeral fit for a king and is even buried with jewelry, riches, and goods in order to win over the gods once he gets to the netherworld.

Once all the funeral rites are done, and the statue is built, an emotionally racked Gilgamesh throws off his royal garments and clothes himself in animal skins. Gilgamesh has lost the one he loved most in the world, and it changes him—he is no longer the tyrant or the epic adventurer he was before. He's driven nearly mad with grief and goes out of the city to wander the world, aimless and without purpose.

Even though Gilgamesh leaves civilization, there is one thought that he cannot escape. Death has become a stinging reality. He begins to think about his own mortality, realizing that he will inevitably also die one day. He thinks, "How can I rest, how can I be at peace? Despair is in my heart. What my brother is now, that shall I be when I am dead?" He begins to feel that there is no point in achievements or merits. Even fame has lost its luster in the wake of mortality.

He becomes so obsessed with the idea of death and trying to avoid it that he is driven to journey to the ends of the earth to find the secret of immortality. He knows of a legendary man who had survived the Great Flood that nearly wiped out all life on the earth. He had heard that this man, Utnapishtim, also called the "Faraway" because he lives far off where no other man has ever been, is immortal and has already lived thousands of years. Gilgamesh believes that because of this, immortality for humans is possible and that he might be able to attain it if he can gain the man's secret.

Gilgamesh begins the long journey and eventually comes to a twin mountain called Mashu, which presents a formidable challenge. The mountain is so great that the tops of its peaks touch heaven itself. The bottom goes all the way down into the underworld. When Gilgamesh approaches its gates, he is met by the mountain's guardians: two scorpion monsters who are husband and wife.

The scorpion man is surprised to see Gilgamesh, telling him no mortal human has ever come that far. He asks what Gilgamesh is doing in such a faraway place, and Gilgamesh tells him of his quest for immortality. The scorpion monster tells him that the immortal man he seeks lives on the other side of the mountain and that it will not be possible to reach him. It is impossible to go over the mountain, but there is a tunnel that runs through it to the other side. The scorpion man informs Gilgamesh that this route is impossible for a mortal man as well. It would take twenty-four hours to go through, and he would be plunged into pitch-blackness—no man could survive it.[55] They tell him for that reason, they cannot let him through. Yet Gilgamesh persists and pleads with them to allow him to pass. Finally, they give in but give him a final warning.

Gilgamesh endures the long hours swallowed up by complete darkness as he makes his way through the tunnel. After twenty-four hours, he makes it to the other side, and what he sees when he reaches the end is stunning. Before him is a beautiful garden, full of fruit and flowers. Beyond that is a vast sea that seems to have no end.

At the edge of the sea stands a barmaid, looking out over the water. Gilgamesh approaches her. She takes in his wild appearance and is frightened at the sight. She flees into the tavern and bars the door. Gilgamesh runs to the door and bangs on it, yelling that he is the great Gilgamesh and that she must open the door or he will break it down. From behind the door, she asks why his appearance is crazy and

---

[55] The literal translation calls it twelve "double hours," possibly a unit of time similar to the ancient Chinese units of time that counted time as double hours. For example, 11 p.m. to 1 a.m. was Rat Hour.

ragged like a criminal. He tells her about his grief and his quest, and she opens the door. She invites him in and offers him food, drink, and clothing, which he refuses. He wants nothing that might distract or delay him in his journey—he needs to find a way across the great sea before him.

The barmaid tells him the sun god Shamash crosses the waters each day, but it is not possible for a man. The waters are too treacherous for a mortal, and even if by some chance he could make it over the sea, he would not be able to make it past the poisoned waters of death. His only chance would be to get Urshanabi, the immortal man's boatman, to ferry him across. Seeing that it is futile to continue to try to persuade him from crossing, the barmaid tells Gilgamesh how to reach the ferryman's house.

Gilgamesh treks through the forest and reaches the house, which is guarded by two stone golems. He foolishly attacks and destroys the stone golems, unaware of their real purpose and importance. The boatman comes out and agrees to ferry Gilgamesh across the waters but tells him the journey will now be more difficult and dangerous. The stone golems, which he had smashed, were used to pull the boat across the sea and protect it from the treacherous waters. There is only one way to get the boat across now.

Urshanabi tells Gilgamesh he must go into the forest and cut down 112 thin trees to use as poles. The poles then need to be fitted with rings and covered in tar pitch to make them waterproof. After Gilgamesh completes the task, the men get in the boat and go on their way. A journey that would take a normal boat two months takes the ferryman and Gilgamesh only three days to make. They cross the great sea and reach the poisoned waters of death. The boatman tells Gilgamesh that he must use the poles to move the boat across the deadly waters, but he must not touch the water. If he does, he will die.

Taking all 112 poles into his arms at once, Gilgamesh puts them in the water and propels the boat. One by one, the poles break. When the last pole breaks, Gilgamesh takes off his animal skin garment and holds it up, creating a sail. The boat finally makes it to the opposite shore, where the immortal man is waiting.

The ancient man is greatly surprised and asks Gilgamesh the meaning of his visit. Gilgamesh tells him about Enkidu and his quest for immortality. Unmoved, Utnapishtim tells him that nothing lives forever and that his grief and obsession with immortality are unwarranted. Persistent, Gilgamesh asks the man if it is possible to gain immortality and, if so, how he can do it.

The old man tells the story of how he became immortal. He says that he was the king of a city that sat on the banks of the Euphrates River. One day, the gods held a secret meeting. During the meeting, the supreme god Enlil ordered that a great flood must be sent to the earth to wipe out all of mankind.

However, the wise god Ea betrayed Enlil and warned Utnapishtim that a flood was coming and that he needed to prepare in order to survive. He would need to build an immense boat with six decks, large enough for two of each kind of living thing on the earth to fit alongside him and his family.

Knowing the boat would raise questions, the old man asked Ea what he should tell everyone about it. Ea ordered him to lie and say that Enlil hated him and that he was being banished. The great flood did come, and after seven days of rain, which wiped out every living thing from the earth, the waters began to recede. The boat came to rest on the peak of a mountain. Not knowing if there was still water around the boat, Utnapishtim let a dove out of the upper windows. Since it found no dry land to rest, it came back. He next released a swallow, which also returned. Finally, he sent out a raven, and the bird did not come back, indicating that the waters had receded. They could safely leave the boat.

Since Enlil had caused the flood without the consent of the other gods, they would not forgive him. The old man and his family left the boat and made sacrifices to Enlil, but when Enlil saw that some humans had survived, he was angry. Ea revealed that it was he who helped save them because he felt that the flood was unfair. If Enlil had wanted to punish the wicked humans, he should have just sent wolves and famine to kill those unworthy of living, allowing the good to survive.

Feeling sorry for what he did, Enlil blessed the old man and his wife, bestowing on them god-like status and immortality for saving the human race. The old man concludes his story by telling Gilgamesh that only he and his wife were declared worthy enough to receive this gift of immortality. Yet Gilgamesh continues to wonder if he could do something to make himself worthy of it as well.

The old man proposes a test, telling Gilgamesh that if he passes, he, too, could receive the immortality of a god. All he will have to do is stay awake for six days and seven nights without falling asleep. He agrees but immediately falls into a deep slumber and stays asleep for seven days. When the old man wakes Gilgamesh, he tries to deny that he fell asleep. But the old man and his wife are smart enough to have proof that seven days have passed. Each day, the old woman baked a loaf of bread. They show Gilgamesh the bread from the first day, now covered in mold, while the new loaf is still fresh. He can no longer deny that he has failed the test, and he sinks into a deep depression, knowing with surety that he will not be able to escape death.

The old man tells Gilgamesh and the boatman that they must leave and never come back. But before going, the old man tells Gilgamesh he needs to clean up his crazy appearance and once again don his royal garb so he can return to the city in honor and not as a madman.

The old woman, feeling sorry for Gilgamesh, asks her husband if there is anything they can give him. The old man tells Gilgamesh that there is a secret of the gods he will give as a parting gift. He tells Gilgamesh that on the bottom of the sea is a thorny plant that, when eaten, can make the old turn young again. Once Gilgamesh and the boatman return to the sea, Gilgamesh is determined to find the thorny plant. In order to reach the bottom of the sea, he ties stones to his feet and gets into the water, where he sinks down, down, down. He finds the thorny plant and takes it, cutting the stones from his feet and resurfacing. He tells the boatman that he plans to share the plant with the elders and the rest of the city so that they can all become young again.

Once on shore, Gilgamesh makes camp for the night. He goes for a swim in the cool refreshing waters nearby but has unwisely left his precious thorny plant unattended. A passing snake smells it and eats it while Gilgamesh swims. When he gets out of the water, he sees that the plant is gone and that a snake is shedding its skin, becoming young again. Seeing his only opportunity for youth gone, Gilgamesh sits and cries.

He returns to the city with the boatman and stands at the gate, showing him the splendors of Uruk. Once he is back at home, he writes the story of his epic journey. Upon his death, the waters of the Euphrates River part, which is where the hero supposedly lies today.

Although the story has all the telltale signs of Sumerian culture, many of the elements are decidedly Babylonian and Akkadian. Proof of heavy Babylonian influence in the writing seems to have been found in an expedition that took place in 1849 CE. An archaeologist, Austin Henry Layard, journeyed to Mesopotamia to find physical evidence of events and people who were talked about in the Bible. What he found was game-changing in terms of ground-breaking literary works.

Among the ruins of the once-great walls of the Assyrian city of Nineveh[56] lay the Library of Ashurbanipal.[57] Among the wealth of historical and cultural knowledge found in its thirty thousand clay tablets of ancient writings was a masterpiece of ancient poetry—the

---

[56] Nineveh was near the modern-day city of Mosul in northern Iraq. The Assyrian Empire collapsed sometime between 612 and 609 BCE.

[57] H. G. Wells called it "the most precious source of historical material in the world."

Epic of Gilgamesh.[58] It is believed that it was written by a Babylonian writer named Sin-leqi-unninni.

Though the writings were dated back to between 1300 and 1000 BCE, well after the Akkadian Empire rose and fell, there was something interesting about the text—it was written mainly in Akkadian cuneiform. While it is probable that many people from several cultures and time periods wrote, rewrote, and added their own touches to the story, the Akkadian cuneiform indicates that at least one version of the epic poem was written during the time of the Akkadian Empire.[59] The words on these tablets reflect who the Akkadians were as a people, how their society worked, and insight into some of their beliefs.

Although Gilgamesh's story is ancient, it has been impactful. It has inspired artists and writers over a vast period of time and cultures, even down to the Greeks and Romans. It was a story that influenced great empires thousands of years after it was first told. But more than that, it gives us insight into the culture, values, and thinking of the Akkadians who told it.

In the story, Gilgamesh is strong, courageous, and well-built—qualities that the culture valued. At one point, the story says he would rather die in glory for killing Humbaba than live without having made the attempt. We can see glory and fame prized, sometimes even higher than life itself. But once Gilgamesh achieves his goal, he does not find himself happy. In fact, once his friend dies, his life is empty and meaningless, despite his glorious adventures.

The Akkadians and ancient Mesopotamian people in general put a high value on social relationships—these were the real prize. They also believed in strong relationships with the gods, whom they believed interacted in their affairs daily. Aside from sensing how the people

---

[58] It is also known as the *Gilgamesh Cycle*.

[59] The epic is believed to have been written between 2150 and 1400 BCE. It was probably written in various parts over time and then eventually compiled into a complete story.

valued fairness and unoppressive rulers—the people of Uruk chastised Gilgamesh in the beginning for his brutish ways—it also showed that they felt that unchecked power wielded with cruelty was not the path to happiness, nor was it a purposeful life.

The Akkadian/Sumerian culture had a vastly different belief system that, for the most part, has not survived time. It was based on a multitude of gods and goddesses who often had reptilian features. The people had less fear of the gods than later civilizations like the Greeks and Romans, as they looked to them more for protection and advice. The story also gives us a glimpse into their views of nature and how it related to their mythologies and pantheons—the sun god crossing the sky, crossing the water as a symbol of transformation, and a snake shedding its skin. The epic tale also gives us an interesting look at their views on sex, which was often part of their worship. These cultural views on sex, prostitution, gods, and nature can be seen in their influence on the Greeks and Romans, who had temple prostitutes as part of their worship and used gods and goddesses to explain nature.

The story also reveals that the people of the time were really not much different than modern humans. They had skilled artists, writers, and craftsmen. The Akkadian Empire had a pretty sophisticated society with a variety of social and economic classes. On an individual level, the people had the same feelings of love, ambition, friendship, loss, loneliness, and revenge as people today. They wondered about their sense of purpose and had a fear of death.

There is another very interesting aspect of the Gilgamesh story, one that also connects with millions of people today. The story of Utnapishtim and a great flood is very similar to what happened to Noah and the great deluge mentioned in the biblical Book of Genesis, an event that is corroborated by geological evidence. According to the chronology of the Bible, the Great Flood would have happened a relatively short time before what historians believe to be the beginning of the Akkadian Empire. So, although Akkadians had changed the events when telling their epic tale, they evidently based it on real events, as many stories and mythologies often do. It is perhaps one of the oldest mythologies connected to the flood.[60].

Gilgamesh, though his story is a fictionalized version of some real people, places, and events, might be the most widely known figure in Akkadian naru writings. But there is another man often connected to the empire whose true name and identity continue to remain a mystery.

---

[60] Scholars have noted that the "Great Flood is the closest thing to a universal story that the human race possesses."

Chapter 9 – "A Mighty Hunter in Opposition to God"

The biblical Book of Genesis refers to this man as "a mighty hunter in opposition to God," while some Jewish rabbinical texts translate his name to mean "rebel." Christian, Jewish, Muslim, and Arabic religious works all mention his name. Intriguing and mystifying scholars and historians for centuries, the true identity of the enigmatic Nimrod has eluded history.[61]

There is no shortage of theories as to his real name and historical identity. Some scholars place him in the time period of the founding of Uruk, even claiming that he was possibly the father of Gilgamesh or the man Enmerkar, the founder of Uruk.[62] Others place him later as a founder of the Assyrian Empire. But numerous scholars place him within the Akkadian Empire, possibly even as a well-known person.

---

[61] There are mountains of theories and thoughts on who Nimrod was, and it is impossible to talk about all of them in one chapter. This chapter is not designed to conclusively prove who Nimrod actually was but rather present evidence, theories, and reasonings that show he existed and why some scholars believe he may have been a ruler of the Akkadian Empire. It is also not intended to promote religious ideas. We are attempting to share information from historical sources, many of which happen to be religious.

But did Nimrod even exist? And what evidence is there that he was part of the Akkadian Empire?

There is a copious amount of evidence to show that Nimrod was indeed a real person. Religious and non-religious texts and traditions (including Sumerian-Akkadian didactic poems) all mention a man named Nimrod. Some suggest that he was no more than a mortal man, while other texts connect him with divinities like the gods Marduk and Bel (and later the Greek Orion).

However, the majority of what is known about Nimrod actually comes from the Bible. Genesis 10:10 says that "The beginning of Nimrod's kingdom included the cities of Babel, Erech,[63] Accad [Akkad or Agade], and Calneh[64] which were located in the land of Shinar [Sumer]." One Bible translation said he "made the start in becoming a mighty one in the earth." The start of what? Perhaps an empire?

With the rise of Nimrod, it is obvious something new was happening. It's mentioned that he had a kingdom, meaning he would have been a king. German theologian Dr. August Knobel dubbed him the "first post-Flood ruler." He was the first of his kind; no one had existed like him before. He united the fragmented city-states of Sumer and consolidated power under himself as the sole ruler. Who else do we know who was a ruler and pioneered the founding of an empire— the *first* empire? None other than Sargon I. The geographical information surrounding Nimrod fits in with the Akkadian Empire as well. But those things in themselves are not enough.

The second city Genesis mentions in Nimrod's kingdom is Erech/Uruk. Is it a coincidence that Uruk was the second city to be conquered by Sargon? Most notably, both Nimrod and Sargon are

---

[62] Historian David Rohl points out that the "kar" at the end of Enmerkar's name means hunter.

[63] Erech is the Hebrew spelling of Uruk.

[64] The Babylonian Talmud correlates it with the city of Nippur or possibly a twin city of Kish.

given credit for bringing Akkad into the limelight, either building it from scratch or building it up from an irrelevant town into a vast capital city.

Many historical and mythological names connected with a hunter are theorized to be Nimrod, but there was obviously more than one hunter in the ancient world. This would have been someone more extraordinary—a man who wasn't just a hunter of animals. Moses, who wrote the Book of Genesis according to tradition, mentions that he was a hunter, had a kingdom, and built cities. If he was merely out hunting for food or sport like anyone else, why would the author feel the need to mention the fact? It wasn't a rare accomplishment. So, it can be concluded that there was definitely something different about him.

McClintock & Strong's *Cyclopedia* fills in more information about Nimrod as a hunter, saying "that the mighty hunting [of Nimrod] was not confined to the chase is apparent from its close connection with the building of eight cities." The Hebrew word for hunter is also closely connected with the word slaughter or slaughterer, a more apt translation for a warrior. The *Cyclopedia* entry continues, "What Nimrod did in the chase as a hunter was the earlier token of what he achieved as a conqueror. For hunting and heroism were of old specially and naturally associated...The Assyrian monuments also picture many feats in hunting, and the word is often employed to denote campaigning...The chase and the battle, which in the same country were connected so closely in aftertimes."

So, hunting in ancient Mesopotamia was not just about chasing animals around with weapons. It was sometimes more broadly associated with chasing men around with weapons as in battle or more extensive military campaigns, much like the one Sargon undertook on his road to conquest. The victory stelae of Sargon show him slaughtering and enslaving captives, which certainly fits in with the picture of a hunter of men, as do the stelae depicting the sheer brutality of the Akkadian army as a whole. It's not surprising that the way an army operates would be a reflection of its leader.

These bits of information do give us the image of a conqueror, one who was not afraid to kill without regret, either in battle or otherwise, to achieve his goal. Having that quality would undoubtedly be essential for one determined enough to create an empire. But four cities hardly qualify as an empire.

The record shows that Nimrod did not just stop with those four cities. Afterward, the Book of Genesis next mentions that he went into Assyria and "built Nineveh, Rehoboth Ir, Calah, and Resen." This was a big enough deal that hundreds of years later, the Israelites knew about it and referenced it. The prophet Micah equated the land of Nimrod with Assyria, indelibly linking Nimrod with not just one or two cities but the whole region.[65]

It's not hard to see the connection to Sargon in all of this. Both Sargon and Nimrod engaged in vast military conquests in the same areas. It is documented that Sargon took his conquering north into the lands of Assyria and made it part of the empire. There are plenty of inscriptions and artifacts that leave no doubt that Sargon made his mark on Assyria.[66] The conquering and building attributed to Nimrod are consistent with the history of the area and of Sargon's doings, and both men had a huge and lasting impact on the region.

One of the most decisive factors for experts who believe Nimrod and Sargon to be one and the same is his family tree. Nimrod was a Cushite,[67] and a number of scholars connect Cush with the city of Kish, saying that the city was named after the man but with a slight

---

[65] Micah 5:6

[66] This is in opposition to his son Manishtushu, whose reign some archaeologists date the inscriptions. But given the wholly unremarkable nature of Manishtushu and his reign, it's highly unlikely he was the one who conquered Assyria. The majority of archaeological evidence points to Sargon as the one who first took the cities of Assyria.

[67] Descendants of Noah's grandson Cush.

twist in the language.⁶⁸ As has been established, Sargon grew up and came to power in Kish, which means he's very closely associated with the city. It might not be the most interesting or compelling bit of information to connect the two, but it adds to the evidence.

It's clear that both Nimrod and Sargon were out for world domination, but Sargon wasn't the only one of his dynasty to have big ambitions. Naram-sin has often been brought up as a likely candidate for the warrior Nimrod, and with victory stelae like the one that depicts him standing on piles of his dead enemies, it's not hard to see why.

Naram-sin expanded the empire even further than his illustrious grandfather had, conquering the known world, at least according to the Akkadians. Inscriptions regarding Naram-sin were found in Assyrian cities, putting him in the right era, location, and dynasty as Nimrod. He also proclaimed himself as "king of the world" and elevated himself to divine status, which fits in with ancient Sumerian legends that link Nimrod to being a god. In terms of who was the more legendary character, Naram-sin certainly outshines his grandfather, making a good case that he was the mighty Nimrod.

The Jewish historian Josephus paints a picture of Nimrod that falls in line with what we know of Naram-sin.⁶⁹ He wrote that, "[Nimrod] little by little transformed the state of affairs into a tyranny, holding that the only way to detach men from the fear of God was by making them continuously dependent upon his own power." It's true that this description could fit either Sargon or Naram-sin, but classically, Sargon is painted as a hero, while Naram-sin is seen more of the impious anti-hero (remember how he allegedly brought down a whole kingdom in "The Curse of Agade?"). The stories that paint him in a

---

⁶⁸ Geographical evidence supports this, such as the location of the Tigris and Euphrates Rivers around Kish.
⁶⁹ Flavius Josephus is considered to be one of the foremost and most accurate sources of ancient history.

bad light might be fictionalized, but there is also a good chance that they have a ring of truth to them.

We also know that Sargon and Nimrod were game-changers, setting an empire-building trend that revolutionized history. As much as Naram-sin pioneered conquering new lands and *claimed* to be the first to conquer certain cities, he was no Sargon. He already started out in possession of northern and southern Mesopotamia. In fact, some of those cities he claimed to have conquered first had already been conquered by Sargon, so he could hardly be labeled an innovator in that area. Naram-sin's reputation as an empire-builder pales in comparison to Sargon, making him a weaker candidate for Nimrod.

The biggest mark against Naram-sin being identified as Nimrod is a big one—there is a time issue.

The cities that have been confirmed by archaeology to have been built by Naram-sin are dated to the end of the Akkadian Empire, which is outside of the range of Nimrod's time. There are no firm dates for when Nimrod lived, but again, only the Bible gives us any clue as to the time period he would have lived in, and the answer lies in a man named Peleg. So, how do we draw a line from Peleg to Nimrod to Sargon?

Like Sargon, Nimrod was not the name he was given at birth but was a name given to him later, a name that would describe the person he became. The Babylonian Talmud pointedly talks about his midlife name change, stating, "Why, then, was he called Nimrod? Because he stirred up the whole world to rebel [*himrid*] against His [God's] sovereignty." *The Jewish Encyclopedia* agrees with that description, with the writings of Jewish rabbis saying that Nimrod was "the prototype of a rebellious people, his name being interpreted as 'he who made all the people rebellious against God." That's quite an infamous legacy. But the important question is, in what way did he rebel, and how is that connected with all this?

Both Christian and Jewish traditions credit Nimrod with building the infamous Tower of Babel, inciting the people to do so in defiance of the Great Flood that had happened only about one hundred years prior. Given all the ziggurat building going on at that time, the tower was likely a large version of those Sumerian-style pyramids. Religious and non-religious sources state that they built a high tower to the heavens to escape another flood. Though the Genesis account does not specifically state that Nimrod built it, it does connect him with a city named Babel. Josephus gives us compelling information on the subject as well.

"Now it was Nimrod who excited them to such an affront and contempt of God...Now the multitude were very ready to follow the determination of Nimrod and to esteem it a piece of cowardice to submit to God; and they built a tower, neither sparing any pains, nor being in any degree negligent about the work: and by reason of the multitude of hands employed in it, it grew very high, sooner than anyone could expect; but the thickness of it was so great, and it was so strongly built, that thereby its great height seemed, upon the view, to be less than it really was. It was built of burnt brick, cemented together with mortar, made of bitumen, that it might not be liable to admit water."

The Talmud and Book of Jubilees agree with Josephus. In fact, Jubilees gives the most detailed account of the building of the tower. Two Sumerian myths also mention this tower. But before it is dismissed out of hand as a legend, it should be noted that the other sources are quite specific and detailed about the building of it—fictionalized legends often do not contain specifics like that. Texts from Naram-sin's son Shar-kali-sharri say that he took up rebuilding the tower, though he, too, did not complete it. Hundreds of years later, Hammurabi of Babylon took up the building of the tower again.[70] Archaeological evidence also supports the existence of the tower.[71] But why couldn't they finish it?

So, if we can establish that the Tower of Babel existed, we have reason to believe that what happened next to stop the building work is based on fact. Genesis 11:7 states that God confused the people's language. Did that really happen, though? Josephus certainly believed so. "When God saw that they acted so madly, he did not resolve to destroy them utterly, since they were not grown wiser by the destruction of the former sinners; but he caused a tumult among them, by producing in them diverse languages and causing that, through the multitude of those languages, they should not be able to understand one another. The place wherein they built the tower is now called Babylon, because of the confusion of that language which they readily understood before; for the Hebrews mean by the word Babel, confusion."[72] Does archaeology back any of this up? Yes, it does.

Clay tablets from the Library of Ashurbanipal in Nineveh, many of which were copies of earlier texts, tell an interesting story that supports a sudden change in languages. A scribe wrote that he was bestowed with a gift from the gods and was suddenly able to read and write in another language that he had never known before. Anthropological evidence also indicates that during the Akkadian rule, there was a sudden shift in the language (writing), one from pictograph images that meant full words to cuneiform syllables. Granted, these cannot be dated, but it does offer some compelling evidence to support the

---

[70] Hammurabi did not complete it either, but Babylonian King Nebuchadnezzar II claimed that he finished it, at least according to the stele he made about it.

[71] Archaeologists have found remains in the ruins of the ancient city of Babylon that they believe to be the Tower of Babel. A tablet found in the ruins showed a relief image of a stepped tower with a person. The inscription underneath translates to "tower [ziggurat] of the city of Babylon."

[72] The original Sumerian word *babel* meant "gate of God," but the evolution of the word's etymology down to the modern-day English word "babble" is associated with confused speech.

Tower of Babel story. And here is where we get to the part about where it connects to Peleg and Sargon.

The Masoretic Text places the year of the Great Flood at 2370 BCE, which is an extremely important piece of information needed to calculate a timeframe for Nimrod. Genesis, for its part, is the only historical account that gives us any indication of when Nimrod might have lived. The post-flood genealogical record of Genesis 11 uses ages, and from there, it can be calculated that Peleg lived one hundred years after that, being born in 2269 BCE. What does an obscure man like Peleg have to do with Nimrod? There is no direct connection between the two mentioned men.

The Genesis account says that Peleg's name meant "division" because "in his days the earth [that is, "earth's population"] was divided." A sudden shift and diversity in languages would certainly cause a great division among the people, and it would also make it hard to build when nobody can communicate with each other. So, if Peleg's name is a reference to that event and if the confusion around the Tower of Babel occurred in his lifetime, it would place the event within the years of Sargon's reign (2334–2279 BCE).[73] In short, genealogical and chronological texts place Nimrod's life within the same years as Sargon's reign.

Granted, it's quite a journey to get to the conclusion, but the evidence and facts had to be established. Personal beliefs aside, religious texts cannot be dismissed out of hand since they do contain historical information that is backed up by archaeological proof. Does it firmly prove that Nimrod and Sargon were the same person? No, but if all the evidence is accurate, it certainly makes him a good candidate.

Whether Sargon was the infamous Nimrod or not, his dynasty was world-changing but short. During the lifetime of Sargon's great-

---

[73] It could realistically be placed within the reigns of his son and grandson as well, but the other information we have fits Sargon better than it fits his sons.

grandson, rebellions, invasions, and other catastrophes spelled doom for the first empire. The end was inevitable.

Chapter 10 – End of the Empire

Around 2217 BCE, Shar-kali-sharri inherited an empire of glittering metropolises, richly laden ziggurats, and wealth due to the extensive trade routes that had been paved before him. He seemed to have it all—an empire at its peak of prosperity. But like all the kings before him, he faced serious problems. Would he be able to keep a firm hold on the empire his father and forefathers had built?

Hemmed in by enemies on all sides, his empire may have glittered, but the situation was far from golden. As great and god-like as his father had proclaimed himself to be, the empire left to his son was riddled with problems and troubles. As the prince of Nippur, Shar-kali-sharri likely had gotten his feet wet as a ruler, but ruling one city was different from controlling a raging empire bursting with rebellions, invasions, and other issues.

Unlike the kings before Shar-kali-sharri, there are only a few inscriptions about the last Sargonic ruler of the empire, but it appears that he didn't have that empire-commanding warrior charisma that his great-grandfather and father had.

The revolting Sumerian cities ramped up their rebellions, and Shar-kali-sharri found himself overwhelmed by them. His inscriptions show that he most likely kicked off the start of his reign by "campaigning against Sumer, in the mountains." That's not to say he didn't have success. He did battle the Gutians, Amorites, and Elamites and came out victorious. Shar-kali-sharri also captured the Gutian king Sharlag and take him prisoner,[74] while in another year, he "imposed the yoke" on Gutium, maybe through taxes or forcibly absorbing them into the empire as a vassal.

But for any victories he had, the celebration was short-lived.[75] Whole chunks of his empire were quickly lost. Those constant wars with the Gutians did not come cheap. In order to fund the defense of the empire, the king had to raise taxes, and to no one's surprise, this was a very unpopular decision. Many of the rebellions that rose up were in cities that were already unhappy with Akkadian control. Adding oppressive taxes pushed them over the edge into outright revolt and cessation from the empire.

One of the biggest blows to Shar-kali-sharri and the empire was the loss of Lagash. The governor of the city, Lugal-ushumgal, had sworn his loyalty to the king as a vassal ruler. He even had it literally written in stone, with the seal stating, "Shar-kali-sharri, the mighty king of Agade, Lugal-ushumgal, ensi of Lagash, is thy servant."[76] But the governor who came after him did not feel that same sense of commitment to the king. Puzer-Mama revolted and took control of the city for himself and started his own (second) dynasty of Lagash kings, once again separating Lagash from the Akkadian Empire.

The state of the empire was quickly disintegrating, and Shar-kali-sharri seemed unable to stop it. City by city, the Sumerians shook off the yoke of Akkadian rule, going back to the days before Sargon when they ruled themselves. As the strength of his reign started to decline, and control of whole regions was lost, he could no longer be

---

[74] The year of this is unknown.

[75] Given the Akkadian propensity for propaganda, it's hard to tell how much truth there was to the inscriptions of the victories or just how successful his military campaigns were.

[76] *Ensi* is the Sumerian word for governor.

considered "King of the Four Quarters," and his title was relegated to the less grandiose "Mighty King of Akkad."

Shar-kali-sharri may have paled in comparison to his illustrious predecessors, but he certainly had his successes. He helped build up the cities of Babylon and Nippur, directing the construction of temples, monuments, and other buildings. He made sure not to neglect the houses of the gods, most notably picking up the work on the famed temple of Ekur in Nippur. Literally tons of precious metals—gold, copper, and silver—were brought in to beautify the temples.

Cylinder seal of King Shar-kali-sharri.

Although Naram-sin and Shar-kali-sharri were able to beat back the constant Gutian hordes trying to invade the empire, they couldn't be held off forever. It's possible the wealth and prosperity of the cities caught their eye (all those gold- and silver-laden ziggurats were surely gleaming in the sun). It would have been too irresistible to pass up. But the conglomeration of tribes from the Zagros Mountains didn't try to take the Akkadian army head-on most of the time. They utilized a more hit-and-run guerilla warfare style, and by the time the Akkadian soldiers could reach the raided towns, the Gutians were long gone.

Even more than the casualties inflicted on the cities, they wreaked havoc by devastating the Sumerian economy. But as the Gutians ramped up the frequency of their forays into Sumer, the situation deteriorated. The constant raiding made travel and even farm work unsafe. When there is no one to work the farms, no one has food, and famines become common.

The people of the empire weren't only suffering due to the famines caused by the Gutians. Archaeologists and paleoclimatologists found evidence that there was a drought around the same time. Thus, weather conditions only intensified the famines and made them more widespread.

Whole cities were abandoned and lay desolate, their mud-brick buildings slowly turning into dust. The empire was on the brink of disaster. If all this—Gutian invasions, famine, cities laid to waste and sitting desolate, and even the rebuilding of Ekur—sounds familiar, it's because it is.

It's the very scenario written about in "The Curse of Agade," and in some parts, it resonates with the "The Legend of Cutha." In the epic poems, the disasters are attributed to the more renowned and often villainous Naram-sin and his uncontrollable ego. The empire-ending events that happened during Shar-kali-sharri's reign would eventually become mixed in with those of other Akkadian kings, most notably his father. In fact, the real-life events became legendary fables for the ages.

An example of this can be seen in the later Babylonian version of events. Even 1,500 years later, the Babylonian Weidner Chronicle gets in on the Naram-sin bashing, saying, "Naram-Sin destroyed the people of Babylon, so twice Marduk summoned the forces of Gutium against him. Marduk gave his kingship to the Gutian force."[77]

Shar-kali-sharri isn't even given a dishonorable mention for what happened under the scepter of his rule. However, his court officials knew the truth about the state of affairs in the empire. If tradition

---

[77] The Babylonian Chronicles, which were written on clay tablets in cuneiform, detailed the major events of Babylonian history.

holds, they were not happy with Shar-kali-sharri's reign either. Allegedly, they struck the king in the head with clay tablets and killed him. Upon his death, anarchy reigned, and the region was plunged into the Mesopotamian "Dark Ages."

Conclusion

Sargon the Great certainly blew apart the mold when it came to Mesopotamian rulers. Even with his humble and somewhat sad beginning, he showed that a man could pull himself up by the bootstraps and climb from the bottom to the top—with a certain amount of ruthlessness and disloyalty most would find distasteful.

The death of Shar-kali-sharri wasn't the final death knell for the empire. Although it was stripped of its former glory, the state managed to keep limping on. Shar-kali-sharri, though, was likely the last to rule over more than Akkad and a few other cities. He had a son, Sharddiqubbisin, who is all but forgotten to history and does not appear to have followed his father to the throne.

In the chaos and anarchy that followed, the *Sumerian King List* mentions four men who competed for the throne in just three years after Shar-kali-sharri's death, none of whom could hold on to power or dominance. With few details to go by, there is some confusion over what happened in those three years. It is possible that a civil war between those vying for the throne broke out. But apparently, the high turnover of rulers was just as confusing to the Akkadians and Sumerians. One inscription from the time asks, "Then who was king? Who was not the king? Igigi, Imi, Nanum, Ilulu: four of them ruled for only three years."

After that quick succession came a somewhat more stable king, Dudu, who ruled the empire for twenty-one years. During his tenure, it seems he may have tried to patch the empire back together, going after cities and regions that had formerly been under Akkadian rule, like Umma, Girsu, and Elam. But the empire was too far gone by that point. The Gutian problem had already brought the empire to near collapse, and any little bit of territory Dudu could gain back couldn't restore it to its former glory.

Dudu's son Shu-turul was the last king of Akkad, with his rule stretching to no more than Kish, Tutub, and Eshnunna. But his rule only led to the imminent and complete collapse of the Akkadian rule. During his reign, the Gutians swept down on the crippled empire in a full-scale invasion, and the demoralized Akkadian army was too weakened to fight them off any longer.

What happened to the empire after the Gutians came is somewhat muddled due to the lack of inscriptions. The Gutians were no Sargonic dynasty. They left no inscriptions, monuments, or glittering temples to tell the history of who they were, but they were probably an underdeveloped civilization compared to the Sumerians and Akkadians. They ended an entire civilization without even knowing how to replace it, as it appears they had no idea what to do with an empire. Famine, death, and disrepair became their legacy.

Their poor rulership and understanding of a complex society created unstable chaos. Only one of the twenty-two Gutian kings who reigned throughout the Gutian dynasty, which lasted anywhere from twenty-five to one hundred years, made it as long as seven years on the throne. Nobody even knows his name. Most only ruled one to two years, with the last one being on the throne for little more than a month. He was only on the throne for a meager forty days.

Sumerian cities cared for the Gutians even less than they liked having Akkadian overlords. For once, the Akkadian cities agreed with them. Even 1,500 years later, the Babylonians were no fans of the Gutians, inscribing on the Weider Chronicle, "The Gutians were unhappy people unaware how to revere the gods, ignorant of the right cultic practices. Utu-hengal, the fisherman, caught a fish at the edge of the sea for an offering. That fish should not be offered to another god until it had been offered to Marduk, but the Gutians took the boiled fish from his hand before it was offered, so by his august command, Marduk removed the Gutian force from the rule of his land and gave it to Utu-hengal."

It was Lagash that kicked off the Gutian expulsion from the region. Gudea, a warrior from the city, rid Lagash of the Gutians and took over as king, rebuilding the wrecked temples and restoring the culture back to its Sumerian glory. He's not named in the *Sumerian King List*, but celebratory inscriptions show that he was fairly impressed with what he did, dubbing himself the "true shepherd" of his people.

Uruk followed the example of Lagash. Utu-hengal freed his city of Uruk from the Gutians, but he wasn't happy to just stop there. He and his army chased them out from the surrounding cities, even as far as Nippur. Uruk became the next regional power, with Ur following it.

The city of Akkad itself did not survive long after the Gutian takeover. They destroyed the once great and proud jeweled capital of the empire. Its destruction was likely a complete one, the ruins of which have never been found. Its location is a mystery that may never be solved.

However, what did remain was a system of government that served as a model for not only future empires of the region but also of the world throughout history. Although the site of Akkad has long been forgotten and covered in dust, its memory stayed alive to inspire Mesopotamian conquerors that followed it. Possibly its greatest post-empire achievements were the births of two successive well-known world powers—the Assyrian and Babylonian Empires.

Here's another book by Captivating History that you might like

Free Bonus from Captivating History (Available for a Limited time)

Hi History Lovers!

Now you have a chance to join our exclusive history list so you can get your first history ebook for free as well as discounts and a potential to get more history books for free! Simply visit the link below to join.

Captivatinghistory.com/ebook

Also, make sure to follow us on Facebook, Twitter and Youtube by searching for Captivating History.

References

"The Akkadian Empire." History on the Net. © 2000-2021, Salem Media. https://www.historyonthenet.com/the-akkadian-empire.

Mark, J. J. (2009, September 02). "Sargon of Akkad." World History Encyclopedia. Retrieved from https://www.worldhistory.org/Sargon_of_Akkad/.

Britannica, The Editors of Encyclopedia. "Tower of Babel." Encyclopedia Britannica. https://www.britannica.com/topic/Tower-of-Babel. Accessed 20 December 2021

Smithsonian Channel via YouTube: "Some Very Compelling Evidence the Tower of Babel Was Real." https://www.youtube.com/watch?v=kgksU2F18lg.

Flavius Josephus. *Jewish Antiquities*, I, 114, 115 (iv, 2, 3).

New World Encyclopedia. "Sargon I." https://www.newworldencyclopedia.org/entry/Sargon_I.

Binkley, Roberta (1998). "The Importance of Enheduanna." https://www.cddc.vt.edu/feminism/Enheduanna.html.

Van de Mieroop, M. (2007). *A History of the Ancient Near East, ca. 3000-323 BC*. Malden: Blackwell.

pp. 68-69.

Britannica, The Editors of Encyclopedia. "Nimrod." Encyclopedia Britannica. https://www.britannica.com/biography/Nimrod.

Poplicha, J. (1929). "The Biblical Nimrod and the Kingdom of Eanna." *Journal of the American Oriental Society, 49*, 303-317. https://doi.org/10.2307/593008.

"Queen Puabi's Headdress from the Royal Cemetery at Ur - Penn Museum." www.penn.museum

Hafford, William B. (2018). "A Spectacular Discovery: Burials Simple and Splendid." Expedition: 62-63.

Lecture on the Epic of Gilgamesh. Andrew George, Professor of Babylonian, School of Oriental and African Studies (SOAS), University of London.

Kramer, Samuel Noah (1973). *History Begins at Sumer.* Doubleday.

Hill, Bryan. "Ancient Origins: The Rise and Fall of Sumer and Akkad." https://www.ancient-origins.net/ancient-places-asia/rise-and-fall-sumer-and-akkad-003192.

S. Wise Bauer (2007). *The History of the Ancient World.* W. W. Norton.

Salive, Natalie. "Lions and Kings: The Transformation of Lions as an Index of Power in the Middle East." https://deepblue.lib.umich.edu/bitstream/handle/2027.42/147390/nsalive.pdf?sequence=1

Sargon & Ur-Zababa ETCSL translation https://etcsl.orinst.ox.ac.uk/cgi-bin/etcsl.cgi?text=t.2.1.4#.

"Sargon's Victory Stele." http://sumerianshakespeare.com/56801/.

Patricia McBroom (2001). "UC Berkeley scholars help translate poems of high priestess whom Assyriologists identify as the first named author in history."

https://www.berkeley.edu/news/media/releases/2001/03/06_poems.html.

"14 Poems of Enheduanna." https://atelim.com/14-poems-of-enheduanna.html.

Foster, Benjamin (2016). The *Age of Agade. Inventing Empire in Ancient Mesopotamia.*

Mark, Joshua J. (2019). "Truth Wrapped in Fiction: Mesopotamian Naru Literature."

https://www.worldhistory.org/article/749/truths-wrapped-in-fiction-mesopotamian-naru-litera/.

Mark, Joshua (2014). "The Curse of Agade: Naram-Sin's Battle with the Gods."

https://www.worldhistory.org/article/748/the-curse-of-agade-naram-sins-battle-with-the-gods/.

"The cursing of Agade: Translation. Old Babylonian version."

https://etcsl.orinst.ox.ac.uk/section2/tr215.htm.

"Nimrod." Insight on the Scriptures Volume 2. Watchtower Bible and Tract Society of Pennsylvania. https://wol.jw.org/en/wol/d/r1/lp-e/1200003259.

Kasher, Menahem M. "Nimrod." Encyclopedia of Biblical Interpretation, Vol. II, 1955, p. 79.

Petrovich, Douglas. "Identifying Nimrod of Genesis 10 with Sargon of Akkad by Exegetical and Archaeological Means."

https://www.etsjets.org/files/JETS-PDFs/56/56-2/JETS_56-2_273-305_Petrovich.pdf.

Levin, Y. (2002). "Nimrod the Mighty, King of Kish, King of Sumer and Akkad." Vetus Testamentum, 52 (3), 350–366. http://www.jstor.org/stable/1585058.

Peleg. "Insight on the Scriptures, Volume 2." Watchtower Bible and Tract Society of Pennsylvania.

NOAA. "Drought and the Akkadian Empire." https://www.ncei.noaa.gov/sites/default/files/2021-11/6%20Drought%20and%20the%20Akkadian%20Empire%20-Final-OCT%202021.pdf.

Cullen, H M, Menocal, P.B. de, Hemming, S, Hemming, G, Brown, F H, Guilderson, T, & Sirocko, F. "Climate change and the collapse of the Akkadian empire: Evidence from the deep sea." United States. https://doi.org/10.1130/0091-7613(2000)028<0379:CCATCO>2.3.CO;2.

Haywood, John (2012). *Chronicles of the Ancient World*. London: Quercus.

Printed in Great Britain
by Amazon